Dear Dan,

I compiled the ideas in this book based on my own experience in the association market and beyond over the last two decades. My hope is that this concept will help you frame the future in a way that embraces the past while exploring new frontiers.

Happy reading!

Amith Nagarajan

Praise for Amith Nagarajan
and *The Open Garden Organization*

As CEO of AIIM, I wrestled constantly with how to better focus my staff and my board—and frankly my own efforts—on what is truly important. Far too often, we would wind up having "traditional" association conversations—responding to the latest chapter blow-up, worrying what to do about member retention, and trying to understand the needs of our most active members. Over time, I realized that in these disruptive times, we had it exactly backwards. The key to the future lay not in deeper and deeper understanding of the core, but on what it takes to engage those at the periphery. Making the association a trusted provider and curator of content is key to engaging those at the edges—tomorrow's new blood—and is critical to making engagement a habit rather than a one-off. Amith Nagarajan's *The Open Garden Organization* is a guidebook that will inspire you to go further than ever before and help you achieve these big goals.

—JOHN MANCINI
Former CEO, AIIM

Amith Nagarajan has combined his work with associations and his experience in building his own company to provide a blueprint for associations to use as they journey into a future that is changing and evolving quicker than ever before. It is a simple message, but one that challenges all of us to adapt to a new way of thinking for associations to remain relevant.

—JOHN GRAHAM
President & CEO, American Society of Association Executives (ASAE)

Amith has an uncanny ability to see and help create the future. That's why I'm both a fan and a follower. See what's ahead in the pages of this book.

—MARY BYERS

Author, Race for Relevance: 5 Radical Changes for Associations

Amith is one of the rare few in the association community who both understands the big changes we're facing in leadership and management today—and can provide useful, tangible advice on how to deal with it. If you want your association to thrive in the next ten years, you'd be smart to keep this book by your side.

—JAMIE NOTTER

Culture Consultant

Co-author, Humanize *and* When Millennials Take Over

Amith challenges association leaders to combine clear purpose, obvious culture, and intentional inclusivity into a model that can propel associations into the next century.

—RON MOEN

Chief Information Officer, American College of Chest Physicians

THE OPEN GARDEN ORGANIZATION

AMITH NAGARAJAN

THE
OPEN GARDEN
ORGANIZATION

A Blueprint for Associations *in the* Digital Age

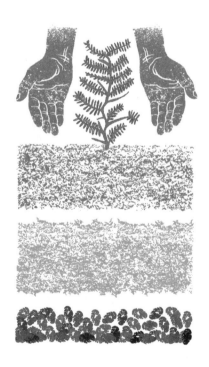

Published by Advantage, Charleston, South Carolina.
Member of Advantage Media Group.

ADVANTAGE is a registered trademark, and the Advantage colophon is a trademark of Advantage Media Group, Inc.

Printed in the United States of America.

10 9 8 7 6 5 4 3 2 1

ISBN: 978-1-59932-955-0
LCCN: 2018943650

Cover design by Wesley Strickland.
Layout design by Megan Elger.

This publication is designed to provide accurate and authoritative information in regard to the subject matter covered. It is sold with the understanding that the publisher is not engaged in rendering legal, accounting, or other professional services. If legal advice or other expert assistance is required, the services of a competent professional person should be sought.

Advantage Media Group is proud to be a part of the Tree Neutral® program. Tree Neutral offsets the number of trees consumed in the production and printing of this book by taking proactive steps such as planting trees in direct proportion to the number of trees used to print books. To learn more about Tree Neutral, please visit **www.treeneutral.com**.

Advantage Media Group is a publisher of business, self-improvement, and professional development books and online learning. We help entrepreneurs, business leaders, and professionals share their Stories, Passion, and Knowledge to help others Learn & Grow. Do you have a manuscript or book idea that you would like us to consider for publishing? Please visit **advantagefamily.com** or call **1.866.775.1696**.

I would like to dedicate this book to my children. Their boundless enthusiasm and energy gives me great hope for a future filled with brightness, joy, peace, and prosperity around the world.

Table of Contents

SECTION III: THE CROPS

About the Author

Amith Nagarajan helps associations, non-profits, and other brands engage with their audiences on a daily basis. Amith founded and grew Aptify into a worldwide leader in Association Management Software and sold the company in 2017 to Community Brands. His newest venture, rasa.io, has developed cutting edge AI to drive meaningful daily engagement between a brand and its audience through personalized content curation. Outside of rasa.io, Amith is an active early stage investor in B2B SaaS companies. He has had the good fortune of decades of success as an entrepreneur and enjoys helping others in their journey. Amith is currently a member of the board of directors for The Idea Village and Align Today. He also is the founder and chairman of the board for AssociationSuccess.org. Amith received his bachelor's degree from California Polytechnic State University-San Luis Obispo and also completed MIT's Entrepreneurial Masters Program. Amith is an active member of Entrepreneur's Organization. Reach out to Amith on LinkedIn or check out www.rasa.io if you'd like to learn more.

The Open Garden Model:
A Summary

Across the globe, associations are facing a questionable future. Waves of major economic, political, and social changes have brought about technological advancements and generational transitions, leaving as many uncertainties as they have opportunities in their wake. Which path an organization takes now largely depends on how it chooses to engage with an era that is increasingly interested in something deeper than numbers and traditions alone. The future cares much more about why and how you exist than what you do or where you have been.

That's good for associations. Since their inception, associations have stood for a common cause founded in support of a collective interest and a will to better the communities, if not the world, around them. Associations have long filled the gaps between government and private enterprise, helping to propel advancements in education, technology, business, medicine, and law. Taking a glance at history, you will find that for nearly every significant stride toward combatting such important social problems as poverty and discrimination, associations have been aiding the push. But now, many associations are teetering on obsoletion after an industry seemingly immune to change began to collide with an age that demands it.

Many associations have been holding their ground against true innovation for years. Scores are losing market share, others are even facing extinction. No matter the industry, when we work in survival mode, we miss seeing the ways in which we could really thrive. For me, progress is the only way to overcome that dilemma.

I grew up in Silicon Valley, a place known today as a kind of start-up capital. The creative passion that thrived there during the 1980s and 1990s instilled in me a lifelong dedication to helping the underdog, as well as an admiration for entrepreneurial culture and the spirit of innovation. I had those ideals in mind when I founded Aptify—a software company specializing in association management—from my college apartment in 1993. I carry those ideals with me to my current work as chairman at rasa.io and Association Success, the companies I invest in, and the non-profit organizations whose boards I commit my time to serve on.

Many of us never had the opportunities that stand before us today, but now we have the ability to do things differently. The tools and knowledge to further our cause in the ways we would have always wanted are within reach, as long as we're willing and able to use them. If your organization can find its true purpose and create a culture that cultivates—not just maintains—growth, then I believe it can maximize the benefits of where business is going. The ever-expanding advantages of technology allow us to reexamine the ways we think about everything from membership models, to organizational culture, to the very purpose of business itself. Associations have the timely opportunity to find smarter, easier, more profitable, and more fulfilling methods to do their work.

This book aims to inspire and educate the association profession as it grapples with new ideas around culture, business models, and approaches to execution, so they can turn the tide and escape the inertia of their past success. My goal is to create a movement that modernizes the philosophies and practices of the association industry, while reviving the way people outside the industry view its purpose and capabilities.

The bedrock of the book is the "Open Garden Model," an equation founded on three main principles: purpose, culture, and inclusivity. I believe associations are uniquely positioned to use their expertise and purpose to engage an audience that cares, one that usually extends much farther than members alone. The Open Garden Model encourages associations to:

- clarify and deepen their purpose;

- redefine and implement a strong culture; and

- shift their business model to one that embraces an inclusive and expansive audience, reaching far beyond the scope of their current membership targets.

The strategies and tools built around these principles allow associations to grow their market exponentially, creating new and sustainable revenue streams all while elevating brand credibility and member loyalty.

Broken into three sections—"The Bedrock" (finding your Core Purpose and defining your Core Values), "The Soil" (constructing and nurturing your culture), and "The Crops" (finding and engaging your community)—the chapters that follow serve as much as a guide to the changes associations currently face as they do a call to change. Each chapter ends with a Chapter Workshop: a series of questions and activities that you can use with your own associations that will help you apply the material to your specific circumstance.

SECTION I
THE BEDROCK

Chapter One

A TIME FOR CHANGE

Those who cannot change their minds
cannot change anything.

—GEORGE BERNARD SHAW

Change. It's an impossible subject to miss hearing about these days. More than ever, our world is moving faster, connecting billions to ideas, products, and experiences capable of traveling around the world in a matter of seconds. Almost overnight, new technologies continue to reshape the way people interact and societies function, altering lives in ways that are both unprecedented and seemingly unlimited. From how we communicate, work, learn, and socialize, to how we do our grocery shopping, almost nothing has been exempt from the impacts of technological advancements.

Discussions around how we will live in the near future are more popular now than perhaps ever before, at least more so than they were twenty-five years ago. Back then, the world was devoid of smart phones and apps; the internet was closer to a digital frontier town of chat rooms and homemade web pages than the thriving metropolis we know it to be today. That once-barren digital space is now among the hardiest manifestations of progress human civilization has ever seen in regards to a platform for further collaborative innovations.

With more people engaging one another on a wide array of topics—politics, society, culture, entertainment, academia, and everything in between—comes an old dilemma in a new form: Who can we trust to keep us informed?

For better and for worse, the Digital Age has left millions sifting through an apparently endless stream of daily information from sources both historically reputable and completely unknown. It's an information overload that has left many feeling so overwhelmed and bewildered, the best solution seems to be throwing up their hands and tuning out.

At the same time, improving the way we interact, work, and lead our daily lives in general ultimately hinges on the willingness to cut loose and explore uncharted territory. Our values and sense of purpose forms the tools we need to navigate the vast number of uncertainties we now encounter every day. Notably, a unique set of Core Values and a meaningful Core Purpose forms the basis of the Open Garden Model for healthy organizational cultures, which I will lay out in this book. It's those tools that offer the best chance— perhaps the only chance—for any of us to discover durable solutions to the problems we face as a faster-moving, faster-thinking, better-connected, global society. The Open Garden Model allows organizations to extend their reach to include and draw new strength from a larger population of supporters within a strong culture built on a meaningful Core Purpose and guided by a unique set of Core Values.

The uncertainty of all the changes in today's world makes it tempting to dismiss the warning signs that organizations need to update their recruitment and retention strategies. It urges us either to keep doing what's familiar because it kind of works, or to become paralyzed by the overwhelming thought of how much we may have to change. Old habits die hard, as they say. Like it or not, though, change is happening everywhere, every day, to everyone.

The mystery of where progress intends to go is surely its most concerning feature, particularly for those accustomed to sure bets and all the comforts that come along with things staying the same. The trouble is, without a good idea of where we are and how we got there, it's going to be much harder to prepare for where we may end up. With that in mind, let's start from the beginning: What are associations exactly, and why are they so important today?

A BRIEF HISTORY OF ASSOCIATIONS

At their core, associations are a collection of people bound together to advance a common cause. They have also been around for a long time. Historians have documented the existence of professional societies and associations throughout much of human civilization's known history. The Canadian Society of Association Executives (CSAE) traces the first scientific society of its kind to a Renaissance-swept Italy, where scholars and teachers there began the Academia Secretorum of Naples in 1560. The Royal Society of London, a leading scientific society known throughout the world, formed in 1662. And yet, old as they are, countless organizations, associations, and societies (or whatever name you prefer for a group of individuals formed around a particular set of ideas, needs, or services) have existed since there was enough people to join them.

The origins of associations in the United States whittle down to just twenty merchants and a pub in pre-Revolution New York. Two hundred and fifty years ago, over a single day in 1768, the merchants met at Bolton and Sigel's Tavern (now Fraunces Tavern) to decide the fate of commerce in what was fast becoming British America's largest trade centers. There, they formed what would become the first known association in the US—the Chamber of Commerce of the State of New York.[1] Their mission was simple, but broad: declaring itself as an organization intent on furthering the business interests of merchants in New York City. However, as the country inched its way closer to the Revolutionary War, the newly formed association split its membership into two groups, presumably to lessen the bruising from internal conflicts. British loyalists went to one branch, American patriots to the other.[2]

When the war finally ended in 1783, associations became an important fixture in developing and maintaining democracy for a new country. One whose incredibly diverse population, wobbly political infrastructure, and comparatively isolated geography posed enormous challenges to the freedom and prosperity its leaders had promised. Order, legislation, national security, and (as the country's first association had feared) a stable and fair economy all teetered on collapse. Organizing individuals based on a common interest, goal, or need became the cornerstone of the young nation's democracy, giving rise to the vital role associations have played in America ever since.

Over the decades, the number of American associations has soared far beyond any fantasy those twenty merchants in New York

---

1   Rines, George Edwin, "Fraunces' Tavern," in *Encyclopedia Americana,* ed. (1920).

2   Joseph Bucklin Bishop, *A Chronicle of One Hundred and Fifty Years: The Chamber of Commerce of the State of New York, 1768-1918* (New York: Charles Scribner's Sons, 1918).

could have conjured up all those years ago. Their number grew alongside the country's steadily increasing population, and with it, the number of purposes for an association to exist. Today, their size and scope range from large and globally impactful associations, such as the American Association of Retired Persons (AARP) and the American Medical Association (AMA), to niche ones like the National Association of Professional Pet Sitters.

According to a recent report from the Center for Association Leadership, there were 66,985 trade or professional associations, and 1,052,495 charitable and philanthropic organizations operating in the United States during the 2013 fiscal year alone.[3] Combined, American associations and related organizations employed more than 1.3 million people[4] and generated an estimated $142 billion in revenue in the same year. As it turns out, strangers joining together to secure and advance something they each value was, and still is, one of the most effective ways to respond to exceptional uncertainty. That may be a win for associations, but it doesn't guarantee their victory. Holes in the very fabric of associations have begun to weaken their usefulness in the eyes of a new age where exclusivity and commitment are often shunned. Replaced instead with a tech-driven preference for crowd-sourced freedom, and all things fast, easy, and cheap.

3 "The Power of Associations: An Objective Snapshot of the U.S. Association Community," The Center for Association Leadership, last modified January 2015, http://www.thepowerofa.org/wp-content/uploads/2012/03/PowerofAssociations-2015.pdf.

4 "Quarterly Census of Employment and Wages," Bureau of Labor Statistics, accessed April 30, 2018, https://www.bls.gov/cew/.

ASSOCIATIONS NOW: WHAT'S CHANGING AND WHAT'S NOT

It may sound dramatic, but more is likely to change about our professional and personal lives in the coming years than will stay the same. Two primary factors are driving those changes: **societal change**, such as dual-income households and a resounding generational transition, and **technological change**. The latter is unquestionably the key enabler for many advancements in our modern work and life, while the former is the evolving face and ethos of the population at large.

Human behavior and technology are now more connected than ever before, with one influencing the other and vice versa. Because of the growing access to what may seem like basic technologies to many of us today—mobile phones, computers, and internet technologies, for example—those who were previously disconnected are now joining the digital information-sharing paradigm by the millions. New worlds have been breached and bridged to old ones, offering innovations to how we involve our rapidly evolving and expanding sectors. We have more choices and greater access to knowledge than any other time in history.

Progression of how we share information is undoubtedly occurring too quickly for some, while shuffling along at a slow and repetitive stride for others. Regardless of its timing, the one thing we can count on is the traditional model for customer recruitment and retention is over for associations and for-profit businesses alike.

If you think about the underlying purpose of an association, they represent a group of people working together to advance something positive for society at large, or a particular profession. With that in mind, associations are invaluable not only to their members, but to the public itself—an idea that many associations would be wise to embrace and expand upon in today's deeply interconnected society.

After all, associations of all kinds really exist to provide just two things: information and connectivity.

On the information side, associations offer members relevant content, whether it's through publications, surveys, studies, articles, or other resources. Just as well, they provide access to training, conferences, and education. On the connectivity side, associations provide a conduit for connecting people within a specific field of interest. In the latter category, it's easy to see that social networking tools like LinkedIn, Facebook, and more specialized tools have created alternative places for people to convene. If you're an accountant, for example, do you need to go to your local CPA society anymore to find other accountants to interact with, or can you do that on LinkedIn? If you're interested in community service, a specific hobby, or profession, can you join a Facebook group to connect with others who share your interest? Unfortunately, those alternatives usually have negative effects on associations in terms of both overall membership and engagement. So, while good for the individual perhaps, it's just one way that technology has created competitive displacement in the social networking and professional networking elements, which associations often rely on for membership incentives.

Gone are the days where we all received the majority of our information from a handful of media outlets. Today, we can connect to thought leaders through blogs, podcasts, YouTube videos, and a countless number of different online media sources. Granted, there is an equally wide range in content quality, but a lot of content is out there nonetheless and most of it is free. In other words, if your only reason for joining an association was to gain access to the latest industry news, there are many other ways that don't involve membership fees and commitments.

If you joined to access continuing education, which is required in many state-regulated fields, you can easily find many high quality continuing education providers outside the association sector. This sudden growth in alternatives is motivating many people to rethink the need for associations to be the center of their professional universe. But does that mean that associations are doomed? Are they no longer necessary, or even useful? Absolutely not. In fact, I'd argue that they are needed now more than ever; they just need to reassert their purpose and learn how to reconnect and engage in new ways with a society in flux.

Scouting the Terrain: Lessons from the Modern Workplace

Perhaps more so than anywhere else, associations can learn how to adapt to society's evolution by examining the changes occurring in the workplace, considering their members are likely spending most of their time at work. Coupled with the existing connectivity, rapidly emerging technologies and a historically multi-generational workforce are changing the landscape faster than we can say for sure where it will take us. But we can predict what it may look like by examining the social and technological trends happening all around us. When we do, sketches of a deeply collaborative workplace begin to take shape. One in which individuals are put ahead of departments, work schedules are less rigid, companies are smaller and more specialized, and a well-articulated sense of purpose enables coherence and creativity to work in harmony across all levels.

The rising popularity of such concepts as social responsibility and conscious capitalism over the last several years has made it clear that many people are seeking to identify purpose in nearly all aspects of their life. Increasingly, if you cannot engage talent and members with something larger than a paycheck, or resources more inspiring and timely than the occasional newsletter or annual conference, then organizations will inevitably find themselves trying in vain to court a disinterested and dispassionate audience. For organizations waiting for the momentum of these changes to blow over, if the present fervor sustains the way experts predict that it will, they may be left waiting in a vacuum for far too long to survive, much less thrive.

Workforce and workplace trends rarely, if ever, return once they change. Until the 1990s, the average professional was able to move from college graduation to a full-time job and build a career with one or a handful of companies until retirement. Workers with a complete lack of impermanence in their career clearly lead a very different approach and mind-set when it comes to work and career building, most often looking for more from their work to help guide them. Where the premise for workers was once to survive the grueling pace and machine-like expectations long enough to cash in their retirement benefits, they now want to actually enjoy their job or career, find a personal purpose in it, and be allowed the freedom and resources to improve. In that way, the very concept of work as a struggle, and a commonly thankless effort, is receiving an inspiring rewrite. And associations are poised to be this transitional period's most influential stewards. They offer credibility and community in a time when both are increasingly elusive, when more than ever their information and expertise could cast them as a trusted curator in the public eye.

Every expert seems to have their own theories around the association's rising challenges when it comes to recruiting and retaining members and talent alike. When I find associations with recruitment and retention problems, the most common reason is failure to establish and articulate a purpose and culture that enables people to connect with the work they do. It's a long and winding path to take, but for associations to succeed in the expanding global market-place, they first need to thoroughly understand both themselves and the needs/wants of their current and prospective members. Further-more, associations need to truly think about their audience beyond members. A far larger audience exists if membership is viewed as a component of the audience, rather than being the audience in its entirety. In short, if a society (and thus the audience engaged with it) is undergoing periods of significant change, then association leader-ship strategies will need to adapt alongside it, if they hope to remain relevant.

Luckily, associations are neither alone, nor are they the most exposed to today's changes. With better research methods and the lessons of experience as our guides, associations are learning from the for-profit sector just how disengaged workers (and customers) are in traditional marketing and management models. The following graphic explains how important an engaged staff and membership are to your organization. On one side of the continuum, you have those who are disengaged. On the other side, you have actively engaged people, with those who are somewhat neutral or marginally active in the middle. The vast majority of people will live on the left-hand side of this continuum, with 10–20 percent disengaged and 70–80 percent passively engaged. In other words, most people inside and outside of your organization are passive. Meaning: they want to read content, watch videos, possibly attend some training seminars and other events, but they will not cross into active engagement. The problem there is that it's the actively engaged member that associa-tions tend to focus on exclusively. However, rather than trying to get people to actively engage, associations are better off figuring out ways to add value to the lives of their constituents while they are still passive or marginally active. If successful, they will convert to being active, but you have to drive value to the passive folks and simultaneously derive value from that form of engagement. Most associations miss this opportunity by undervaluing passive members and potential members by focusing solely on members who are actively engaged.

Another key in the rules of engagement that's often overlooked is frequency. In his 2013 book *Hooked: How to Build Habit-Forming Products,* author and consultant, Nir Eyal, points to the overwhelming research in social sciences that show how one has to drive frequency in order to facilitate the formation of habit. The more you do something, the more likely it's to become habitual. Eyal says that external and internal triggers—whether that's a smell or sight, or the emotions we feel from winning or losing a game, for instance—drive our desire to either engage or disengage. That is a critical concept for associations. To be a voice people listen to regularly in a profession or field, you have to hook them, and that is what the frequency of engagement is partially responsible for doing. The goal isn't just to get more people to engage with the organiza-

The challenge for associations is most don't have a good reason to frequently engage. They are good at deeply engaging on an infrequent basis, but don't often have enough content to reach their audience daily, weekly, or even monthly, in ways that the recipient wants.

tion, but to get them to engage more often as well in hopes of becoming a habitual source for a variety of resources. The challenge for associations is most don't have a good reason to frequently engage. They are good at deeply engaging on an infrequent basis, but don't often have enough content to reach their audience daily, weekly, or even monthly, in ways that the recipient wants. Many associations do indeed communicate frequently, but are often sharing information of interest to the association staff, not so much to the interest of each individual member.

It takes about six months of intense work for an organization to form a habit. So, let's say you want to roll out a new set of Core Values at the beginning of a given year. That exercise needs to be followed by six months of intentional programming of activities, things that you're doing to reinvigorate those Core Values within your team before they really become part of the fabric of the organization. That's because habits take anywhere from four to six months at the individual level to take root, forming through repetition. You can spend two days talking to me exclusively about culture and values. But after those two days, if we don't talk about values frequently, I'm not going to form a habit around the organization's values. That doesn't mean that after six months your organization is going to have its values rippling through every corner of the organization. It can take years to turn values into habits, but it takes at least six months of very intentional effort to launch your Core Values, or any other major organizational change.

While the estimated $450 billion in lost productivity of such a disengaged workforce is nothing to shrug our shoulders at, pondering the impact that a largely uninterested membership has on the association's growth and capabilities is even more disturbing. It's not a stretch to assume that an apathetic organization won't be inspiring people to make great products, much less develop an excellent service, anytime soon. To make matters worse, the age of social media and billion-dollar start-ups born from garages and dorm rooms is no time to be average.

The marketplace has evolved as well, adapting to the social, political, technological, and economic changes that ripple across one another in ways they never could until now. Corporations now vie to gain the loyalty of consumers and employees alike in a time when both are more confident in their independence—whether it stems from the self-empowerment of technology, the survival of an experience feeling very much like betrayal, or both. But so far, major corporations are meeting their demands in boldly creative ways, paving the path for unprecedented advancement in organizational management, marketing techniques, and business strategies overall.

Despite the trials ahead, it's far from a doom-and-gloom forecast for traditional organizations. An abundance of tools, resources, exceptional talent both young and old, and new frontiers of commerce and opportunity lay before them. This isn't the first time organizations (whether associations or corporations) have found themselves at something of a revolutionary crossroads. And today's public is certainly not the first to endure significant generational maturation during a societal and technological overhaul either, nor will they likely be the last. Reflect on the transformations brought on by previous technological strides—from the first wheel on earth to the rise of agricultural and industrial machines—and you'll find familiar scenes peering back at you.

No organization will be alone in trying to adapt to the changes, and the collective experience has already offered plenty of examples to follow. The principles and ideas of adapting to and implementing change in this book will help guide the path you want to take toward discovering, or rediscovering, a purpose that works for your organization.

Rules of Engagement

As Eyal and others have pointed out in greater detail, engagement is driving a new vision for the almighty rules of yesteryear. Organizations are learning that in order to track, engage, and retain members, you have to change the way you think about rules and those who must adhere to them. In other words, engagement is in, and the rules—while not out—are changing dramatically.

What is disengagement, exactly, and what causes it? Gallup breaks engagement down into three categories: **Engaged**, **Not-Engaged**, and **Actively Disengaged**. According to Gallup, engaged people feel a profound connection to their organization. Those who are not engaged, on the other hand, invest a minimal amount of time to the organization, and put little to no energy or passion into it.

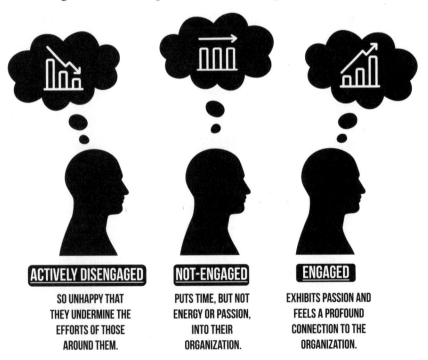

ACTIVELY DISENGAGED
SO UNHAPPY THAT THEY UNDERMINE THE EFFORTS OF THOSE AROUND THEM.

NOT-ENGAGED
PUTS TIME, BUT NOT ENERGY OR PASSION, INTO THEIR ORGANIZATION.

ENGAGED
EXHIBITS PASSION AND FEELS A PROFOUND CONNECTION TO THE ORGANIZATION.

For associations, engagement is about monitoring the all-important recruitment and retention equation. Conference attendance, online forum activity, social media followers, and web traffic all help gauge member engagement. But they don't necessarily correlate to renewals, new memberships, or advancement of the underlying mission. Associations require a more thorough investigation into why and how members are engaging with them, as well as defined goals around what they hope to achieve from that engagement. What are your members curious about? What activities are they most interested in? What types of products, services, or information do they desire most and why? Where do they go most often for these products, services, and information? What problems are they most concerned by? The answers to these types of questions provide the first step in recalibrating what engagement actually means and where and how you can improve your results.

Rise of the People Advantage

The primary benefit to a more engaged membership base is one that is proportionally more productive, of course, but even that idea has its roots elsewhere. If we look at corporations, a continued rise in significance from factors such as steepening global competition, technological advancement, and shifts in social views and realities, have all contributed to a fracturing of large corporations—a phenomenon associations could learn from. Twenty years ago, for instance, there were roughly four million companies in America, employing some 200 million people in total. Today, there are an estimated twenty-eight million companies in operation, most of them niche-focused entities employing a small team of closely aligned, purpose-oriented team members.[5]

As businesses shrink and further specialize, the idea of truly treating customers as individuals with specialized wants, needs, and abilities, is helping to drive some of the shift in the way Americans think about businesses in general. When it comes to membership-based business overall, Americans appear to care about looser commitments, as evidenced by the recent surge in short-term subscription services (such as Netflix, Dropbox, Spotify, and others that one in ten Millennials currently spends roughly $200 per month for[6]), and brand organizations that cater to a specific lifestyle, such as REI, Blue Apron, or even Apple and Nike.

In the 1980s, joining a health club typically required a sign-up fee along with a year or longer commitment. These days, most fitness clubs allow people to go month-to-month, and in some cases, simply use a facility on a day-pass basis. A platform called ClassPass is another good example in this particular industry. Instead of signing up for a particular gym or fitness studio, ClassPass allows someone to access a wide array of classes across many gyms in their home area, or when they travel. The key idea here is that flexibility needs to come first. These days, commitment comes through habit rather than by contract. Habit is built by repetition, and repetition only forms where the greatest value lies.

Choices are greater than ever and consumers, whether professionals in a given field or consumers buying a gym membership, are able to set the terms of how their relationship with any organization

5   "Frequently Asked Questions," SBA Office of Advocacy, last modified September 2012, https://www.sba.gov/sites/default/files/FAQ_Sept_2012.pdf.

6   Brionna Lewis, "It's Not Avocado Toast Draining the Pockets of Millennials, It's Subscription Services," Instamotor, accessed April 30, 2018, https://instamotor.com/blog/monthly-subscription-costs.

begins and evolves. Smart organizations are embracing this idea by offering multiple ways to engage, allowing the casual and uncommitted user to easily start, while finding ways to bring those who have shown a repeat interest in their offerings closer.

Technology has allowed us to live in a world that is nearly borderless, giving people a wide range of choices for their products, services, information, and even social interactions. As a result, people today want less commitment up front. They desire fewer rules, faster results, and more fluidity in how, when, and where they engage with a particular organization or person. Membership scares them away when presented too soon. Look at Amazon as another example, which lures people into membership incrementally by experiencing value first-hand. Over time, this value accretion drives repeat visits/interactions that, in turn, lead to a willingness and desire to commit to a deeper relationship with the organization, like membership. The strategy is clearly paying off. In April 2018, Amazon's founder and CEO, Jeff Bezos, announced in his annual letter to shareholders that Amazon has more than 100 million paid Prime members globally. These Prime members not only pay Amazon $99/year for their membership, but on average spend an additional $1,300 per year on the e-commerce site.[7] That kind of growth is even more impressive when considering that Amazon only launched its Prime Membership program in 2005. It is also important to note that Amazon started business in 1994, so it took them eleven years even to launch their membership program.

Perhaps central to that growth is the organizational culture, having revealed more of its influence on recruitment, engagement,

---

7   Amit Chowdhry, "Amazon Hits Over 100 Million Prime Members," Forbes, last modified April 19, 2018, https://www.forbes.com/sites/amitchowdhry/ 2018/04/19/amazon-prime-100-million-members/#160ebc735433.

and retention in recent decades. People want to feel as though they really *know* an organization, and they want to see if the organization knows them, too. Their answer lies in how well an organization caters to the needs and wants of their lifestyle, even as they change quickly. The benefit there is that culture is a constant within the organization, spanning changes in strategy, environment, and everything else. For an organizational culture that draws in top talent and loyal members, leaders have learned that they must first determine their own values and purpose in accordance with the kind of people they want to attract. That set of values and sense of purpose need to be clear in all of the organization's messages to define themselves coherently and reinforce the organization's identity continuously.

The more we learn about engagement, the clearer the correlation between culture and productivity becomes. But engaging members also requires strong resources (e.g., exclusive studies, noted experts, relevant news content, among others) that are capable of explaining what's going on in the members' field of interest. In other words, tracking and accurately predicting the needs, interests, and future goals of your members is vital to understanding how you can better engage them. The more valuable their membership is to them, the more engaged they will be. Interestingly, with interests changing faster than ever today, it is harder to predict where your audience will want to engage even in the near future. For this reason, it is more critical than ever to find ways to interact with your audience frequently to gather real-time insights into the trending and likely future

> *In other words, tracking and accurately predicting the needs, interests, and future goals of your members is vital to understanding how you can better engage them.*

interests of the group. These improved insights will allow an association to better plan its blog content, conference sessions/speakers, planned publications, and educational courses.

Above all, for any association to engage their members they first have to know who their members are. That means leaders must learn a number of things about their members, such as their strengths, weaknesses, problems they face, and what they need help with in order to resolve them. A key challenge here is that most people often don't know the answer to the questions associations need to ask. When an organization surveys its members, the feedback they receive is inherently "rear-view mirror" insights. That is, people are thinking about where they have been and what they have done. People are generally terrible at forecasting the future for themselves or others. This is why predictive intelligence technology is so important when looking ahead. By looking more at the behaviors of a member or user, an organization can use tools to predict their future interests more accurately than by looking at the rear-view mirror feedback that typically comes from survey results.

Associations can only fully engage the type of member that is in line with their current culture. But as the societies that produce their members progress, the association must also keep in step. And therein lies much of the problem. For an organization wishing to redefine its existing strategies and culture, complications in coordinating internal changes with external needs creates big challenges. Associations often struggle to loosen the fixed structures of their past to adapt their values and purpose to an ever-evolving present, subsequently losing touch with the members they want to keep and attract.

Organizations have begun prioritizing values like respect and trust in increasing numbers and, like all values, they should be clear in membership outreach as well as internal and external messages to management, members, clients, staff—everything should be resonating the same message. Values, as we will discuss later, must be unique and really be part of the organizational DNA. Using generic values doesn't leave a lasting impression or help people understand you. Organizations that succeed in making their unique values central to their cultural identity gain a significant engagement advantage among today's audience, transforming customers and employees into members, and members into proud advocates.

Technical Difficulties

Questions arise over not only why members are not engaged, but also who they are and what they want in the first place. According to a 2017 study conducted by Community Brands, the source of much of the disconnect between members and their organizations may be technology.

The report found that members of professional organizations were much more satisfied if they felt their organization was an "early adopter" of technology, indicating a correlation between loyalty and technology. Unfortunately, only 26 percent of respondents rated their organization as "excellent" on technology use, and just 25 percent felt "extremely connected" to their organization and the work it does.[8] Just one third of members thought their organization was an "early adopter" of technology, while 30 percent of staff believed their organization's adoption of technology "lagged."

Researchers found a significant gap in digital behavior between members and their organizations as well. Eighty-three percent of members had a paid online subscription, such as Amazon or Netflix,

---

8   "Digital Member Study: Examining the Gap Between Member Expectations and Association Technology," Community Brands, accessed April 30, 2018, http://img. en25.com/Web/Abila/%7B41b0cf10-f37e-401c-982c-4b8c52b7e858%7D_2017Di gitalMemberStudy_Report_121317.pdf.

and the same number reported using a smartphone every day. Nearly half had used an app or website to meet people. The vast majority of organizations (76 percent) employ an email marketing platform, but members were less interested in connecting through emails than they were a website with a member portal (53 percent vs. 59 percent). And even though 63 percent of members (74 percent for Millennial members) reported that technology played a "big role" in their daily life and nearly all respondents admitted that technology at least played "some role," the majority of organizations surveyed believed that they were not "technologically advanced or even technologically prepared for the future and able to meet members' expectations."

Only a quarter of those organizations had plans to increase their technology investments in the future.[9]

Gaps in technology adoption weren't the only problem. The study also found that while the majority of organizations believed personalization makes members feel more engaged, most "don't put enough emphasis on creating a personalized experience with recommended content that members value."[10] Personalization, as it turns out, factors significantly into member loyalty. Although only 33 percent of members reported feeling like their organization personal-

Personalization, as it turns out, factors significantly into member loyalty. Although only 33 percent of members reported feeling like their organization personalized content for them, the more than 60 percent of members who felt "extremely connected" to their organization believed they were receiving personalized content.

9   Ibid.

10   Ibid.

ized content for them, the more than 60 percent of members who felt "extremely connected" to their organization believed they were receiving personalized content (recorded as "things they may be interested in, recommendations, and discounts").[11]

CATCHING UP TO THE PROBLEMS

What provides a substantial push to ask for more often comes from an organization's unwillingness to give, to flex and work with the evolving needs of their member and staff base alike. Many organizations are still operating with old bylaws and internal structures, mind-sets, and practices that fail to capitalize on the opportunities the modern world is offering, hampered instead by routines that, while familiar and safe, offer very little flexibility to the process of ingenuity. And, without the ability to innovate, adapting to change in order to secure stability and growth is a futile effort.

That rigidness leads to a lot of friction against the speed of change today and the needs of the society that must respond to it. When we consider numbers like 48 percent of married couples now represent dual-income households[12], and more than 40 percent of households with children under the age of eighteen are primarily or solely supported by working mothers (compared with 11 percent in 1960),[13] a picture emerges of a society whose home and professional needs deviate substantially from previous decades.

Organizations, both associations and for-profit companies, have been mostly local or regional throughout their history as well.

---

11   Ibid.
12   "Economic News Release," Bureau of Labor Statistics, last modified April, 19, 2018, https://www.bls.gov/news.release/famee.nr0.htm.
13   Mark DeWolf, "12 Stats About Working Women," US Department of Labor Blog, accessed April 30, 2018, https://blog.dol.gov/2017/03/01/12-stats-about-working-women.

Beginning in the 1960s, many of the larger corporations went international to at least some degree, but not on the scale that we see in today's globally connected environment. As a result, the message was more controllable in the pre-social media era—even a decade ago, a press release or newly announced mission statement greatly mattered. It allowed an organization to control nearly everything that was said about it, but now every employee, every customer, virtually anyone, can say anything they want about an organization, and hundreds of millions can hear it. In that way, how an organization presents itself to the public is increasingly out of their control, a fact that demands a lot of adjustment for organizations, especially in terms of engagement.

To engage staff and members in the best way possible these days, you have to treat them as an individual to understand their needs; otherwise, the masses are probably going to hear about it. To keep up with the shifting mind-set that such a loss of public perception has afforded, the way people interact with an organization must allow for more customization. In order to leverage their full engagement potential, management structures should be designed to incorporate the strengths, and aid the weaknesses and working styles of their staff and members.

Diversity and Inclusion (D+I) is another key concept in contemporary, well-meaning organizations who seek to build structures that allow everyone to participate and share their voice, regardless of the unique aspects of their individual background and way of life. I believe that a well thought-out and executed D+I strategy is a critical part of any organization, not just associations. At the same time, I push hard for organizations to remember that, while equality and openness are critical inputs into making an organization one that we want to be part of today, the hidden benefit of this is **Diversity of Thought**.

Diversity of thought is the "killer app," if you will, of the D+I movement. Think of D+I in all of its forms, around race, gender, religion, lifestyle preferences, and so on, to be the platform for the way an organization must operate. The outcome, or "app," that D+I produces, if done well, is an incredibly diverse set of ideas. If you foster this in a true way, and are not simply checking the box when it comes to your D+I approach, you'll find that new ideas come at you faster than ever before. The world we live in is better connected with a global, massively diverse audience. To maximize opportunity while best serving our purpose on a global level, D+I must be a central part of our strategy.

Demand Diversity in Thought

We demand all of our team members seek out ideas beyond their own. Diverse ideas often come from diverse people and sources, be creative and seek to turn over stones and coax out ideas from people who may not always be first to share them.

Leadership also benefits by recognizing that their staff and members have different work and life circumstances today, whether it's kids, elderly parents, or even a personal hobby like marathon running. By knowing your staff and members more thoroughly, you can better meet them where their interests, needs/wants, sense of purpose, and skills intersect with the organization's. And while understanding the individual and customizing content has morphed to a more empathetic form of leadership, it doesn't come at the expense of profit. Quite the opposite, in fact, as the real and perceived value of membership actually expands through personalization. What's more is that the people who are motivated by the work of an organization typically stay the longest and are the most involved. Last, but certainly not least, engaging your audience through their emotional connection drives a desire to frequently interact, which also helps form habit—that key component to maximizing revenue generation with the individual and with their network of aligned friends and colleagues. Without the emotional connection forged through common purpose and values, individuals are rarely motivated to engage in this way.

Leaders who employ a customizable approach to engage their staff and members aren't constructing an organization devoid of identity or credibility, either. They are creating a framework that guides, directs, and creates enough space for people to better connect with their work. It's all based on the premise that people will actually be more loyal to a group once they discover what inspires them about its purpose, and what they stand to gain from its work. Sometimes that means leading them by the hand; sometimes that just means getting out of their way. Either way, you can't know how to give someone an ideal experience if you don't first know who they are, and, more importantly, who you are as an organization.

CHAPTER WORKSHOP

» Define what your organization is by identifying why it exists and how it contributes to a larger purpose.

» Establish what you can articulate about your organization's values and purpose that will engage the workforce.

» Understand that your organization's values and purpose shape an organizational culture that will attract similarly aligned members, clients, and staff. That culture should resonate throughout every aspect of the organization from the top down.

For more on engagement, view the eBook, *Scoring Member Engagement*, I wrote on the subject while in my position as CEO at Aptify: https://www.philaculture.org/sites/default/files/scoring_member_engagement.pdf

SUGGESTED READING

Hooked: How to Build Habit-Forming Products by Nir Eyal

Chapter Two

WHY ARE YOU HERE?

"If you want to build a ship, don't drum up people to collect wood and don't assign them tasks and work, but rather teach them to long for the endless immensity of the sea."

—ANTOINE DE SAINT-EXUPÉRY

To make positive change possible, associations need to first know where they're going. The problem is, that can't be determined until they know both where they currently are and exactly why they're trying to go anywhere at all. Change is hard and painful, so it must be seen as something that's so important that it overrides the temptation to stay safe and comfortable. To move an organization forward, everyone must understand and believe in the organization's fundamental purpose. I don't mean it's day-to-day purpose of fulfilling specific tasks to meet a particular goal. I mean its fundamental and ideological purpose, which we'll refer to as **Core Purpose**. That means going deep into the identity of the association, and not just by asking who you are, either. After all, you can't know *who* you are until you know *why* you are here.

Everyone in the association must ask themselves why the organization exists so often that the answer is ingrained in every decision they make, large and small. Once they do, it's possible to navigate the uncertainties of change as a unified group. In associations, it's critical to align this thinking with staff, volunteer leadership, membership, and the public.

Core Purpose is a navigational device, the North Star against which every choice should be measured. It tells everyone, inside and outside the organization, why they are there. It tells them why they should care about the organization's work, offering to them something bigger than themselves—that just being a part of it's a reward. It shouldn't just explain an organization's particular function or goals; it should inspire them. While the organization's values instruct how everyone should behave daily (similar to having a handful of parenting rules, as pointed out by Verne Harnish in the book *Scaling Up: How a Few Companies Make It ... and Why the Rest Don't*), Core Purpose tells them why they should be there in the first place. It should inform everything the organization does, from the high-level planning at the top, to the seemingly mundane tasks at the entry levels. That collective purpose provides the answer to every dilemma people may face, whether as an individual or as an organization. If it aligns with your purpose, if it supports your very reason for being, then do it. If it doesn't, don't.

I know what you're thinking, and you're right. It's not as easy as it sounds. Discovering, or even reaffirming Core Purpose requires a great deal of reflection and a willingness to embrace some level of risk. Neither is easy, but if growth is what you're after, they are only ways to get there.

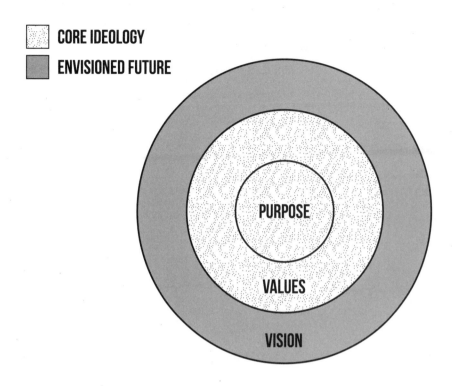

CORE IDEOLOGY
ENVISIONED FUTURE

PURPOSE

VALUES

VISION

SMALL STEPS AND SHORT FALLS: THE PRINCIPLES OF TAKING RISKS AND CULTIVATING EXPERIMENTATION

Most associations suffer from analysis paralysis. That's a phrase you have probably heard more times than you would like. Unfortunately, and as much as I wish it was not the case, it's the truth. The culture of associations, in general, needs to embrace a willingness to experiment, fail, and learn from failure. The reason is fairly simple but incredibly important.

If you're risk averse, often you will be discouraging members and staff from taking risks, trying new things, listening to new ideas, and pushing the organization and its work toward *better*. That's the ultimate purpose of associations, after all, to make a field of study, industry, place, or people better, to put our heads together in the pursuit of advancement. Can that be done if people are so afraid of their ideas and efforts failing that they choose instead to say and do nothing? Success often breeds contentment, which makes it harder to seek higher levels of success. As Jim Collins puts it, "Good is the enemy of great." If you've achieved good results, it is often hard to risk those successes by trying to raise the bar and go for great. Fear of failure isn't evident in startups nearly as much as successful and mature businesses and associations.

Culture of Experimentation:
Encourage innovation by taking small, measured risks when trying new ideas first. Measure the outcome, and then iterate until you achieve the desired results.

If I had to share just one piece of advice with any organization at any stage in its life, it would be to experiment more. Experiment a lot more. What slows so many associations down is that they want to study everything. It's not that they are anti-change necessarily. It's just that they are so risk-averse that they create more risk to themselves by analyzing every decision for a very long time. Rather than making small, incremental changes, testing them out, and seeing what happens through actual results, they theorize the changes until it's too late to make them, or the changes are no longer unique, innovative, or as impactful. They spend a lot of time just thinking about it, talking about it, and, six months later, nothing has happened. Twelve months later, still nothing has happened.

An attitude that encourages experimentation requires only a few things. One, you need to assert the "willingness to fail" mentality that we discussed earlier. You need that attitude deeply embedded into the thought process of the entire organization. That means you can't go around telling people that the organization "prides itself on success." That's one of the most flawed statements to embed into your culture. First, it's generic. The principles built around your purpose need to be unique to your organization. And if you say that one is to be successful, well, is there any organization on planet Earth that doesn't want to be successful? No organization desires failure, but the most successful ones are willing to take risks, absorb, learn from failures, and then drive hard to a better long term result. If short term success is demanded at all times and failure is viewed as toxic, then the team is going to do the things they know are unlikely to fail, and that causes you to repeat the past rather than looking to the future.

Experimentation is required to drive change because it forces you out of your comfort zone and into your growth zone. It forces you to try things that are different from what you have done before and to examine the incremental change. But before anyone can feel comfortable taking risks and experimenting with ideas, they have to know that it's safe for them to fail. This demands an organization to prioritize strategies meant to cultivate vulnerability in their staff and members, because an experimentation culture without vulnerability doesn't lead to true introspection and learning.

> *If short term success is demanded at all times and failure is viewed as toxic, then the team is going to do the things they know are unlikely to fail, and that causes you to repeat the past rather than looking to the future.*

Building such a culture must start from the top. To expect people throughout an organization to show their vulnerability when the top leaders are deemed infallible is unrealistic. Most top leaders claim they are open to feedback but when they actually receive critical feedback, they rarely listen actively and take the input into consideration. At my old company, Aptify—a software company focused on association management—we were challenged in this area. I built Aptify up rapidly and with no outside resources of any kind. I was very young when I started. After the initial startup period, the company took off like a rocket and was extraordinarily successful for many years. The success got to me. I always prided myself on being a leader who took input from the team and focused on innovation. However, roughly ten years into the business, I realized that we had strayed from those roots and were making the same mistakes many other established and successful leaders were making: we were not embracing vulnerability and living our value of innovation.

We decided to change this by displaying failure and celebrating it. Over a period of several years, our leadership team was a broken record in embracing small failures where we learned a new lesson. I spoke about all of the things I had messed up along the way and what I learned. Key team members who had built the company alongside me took the stage at our company's annual internal conference and shared their greatest failures. While entertaining in some ways, the point of these exercises was to show the team that even the most senior roles were not only prone to failure, but they actively sought it out in order to learn and grow. The shift we made at that point in our business was critical to rebooting and reinvigorating our culture, which in turn led to many years of incredible growth, cultural and financial success, and ultimately led to the business being acquired in a strategic deal.

In an environment where people feel comfortable talking about their failures and showing their vulnerability to risk, a feedback loop opens up that makes experimentation useful. If you're not willing to be vulnerable and encourage others to experiment, then people are going to search for theoretical success rather than trying to figure out what's actually happening. The trick is that when you fail, you fail in the pursuit of something good, and you fail differently than how you might have failed before. All that's important is that people learn from failure and share that knowledge with others. The hope is that the next time they or their colleagues fail, they don't fail the same way. You don't want to encourage failure the same way over and over, nor do you want failure to be for lack of effort or insight. You want to encourage trying something new that advances your goals, and if it fails from time to time, that's not only okay, but also something you should consider a win. It's a win because you learned something new that makes you smarter, faster, and more agile.

Advances that have occurred throughout human history in fields as diverse as science, literature, art, and exploration have not taken place because folks were content with repeating the past. They sought to experiment, to seek new knowledge, and to find new and better ways forward. Today is no different. Associations are no different. To meaningfully advance, we must be willing to embrace failure as a way to learn and improve.

But a culture of experimentation needs fail-safes in place, too. A willingness to fail doesn't mean put all of your members and colleagues on Elon Musk's latest rocket and see if they'll get to Mars in one piece. That's not the type of experimentation I'm talking about. I'm talking experimenting in small, incremental ways that allow you to test the waters, so to speak, before you dive in. I'll digress for just a moment to give you a real-life example.

When I founded rasa.io, my goal was to become the go-to AI company for the association industry. Soon after, rasa.io developed a new form of artificial intelligence to automate the creation of a personalized news brief. We pitched it to a number of association CEOs on the basis that it was an effective tool for driving daily, personalized engagement with their members, or their audience in general. The best way to get started, we told them, was to take a very small subset of their audience and do a pilot test with them. We sent news briefs to less than 10 percent of their membership for six weeks. Then we looked at what the data told us about user habits, interests, etc. Rather than thinking about it for months and months, we said, "Let's just try it out, and see how well this new artificial intelligence works to deliver more value to people's inbox every day."

Many people responded by saying something along the lines of, "Oh, I don't know if I can do that. That's kind of risky for me to send this thing out to that many people. Could we send it to ten people instead?"

The problem with that is you're not going to get any meaningful data from a sample size that small. Experimentation has to be implemented in doses that are small enough not to do irreversible harm but large enough that the effects are measurable. It's akin to the idea of trying new foods: you can't form an accurate opinion about a particular dish if you just drag the tip of your pinky finger across it or do nothing more than sniff at it. You have to take at least a couple full bites to judge how it tastes and whether or not you like it. The same goes for experimenting with changes in the organization. Experiment in small, but meaningful doses, preferably with ideas or tools that pose little to no financial risk up front and are low-risk in terms of negative potential impact.

In their book *Great by Choice*, bestselling author, Jim Collins, and business consultant and professor, Morten Hansen, present the idea of small experimentation in a powerful metaphor. They call the concept "Fire Bullets, Then Cannonballs," explaining that you first fire bullets (low-cost, low-risk, low-distraction experiments) to learn which ideas will hit the mark and which will miss. Then, once you have calibrated your line of sight, you fire a cannonball (allocating more resources to your previous, successful effort). Calibrated cannonballs correlate with outsized results; uncalibrated cannonballs correlate with disaster. Extrapolating small, successful ideas (bullets) into huge hits (cannonballs) has a much greater impact than does innovation for the sake of innovating.

That kind of small-scale experimentation is incredibly important toward easing the organization into an Open Garden-based culture because you're able to learn from the experience on a dynamic level, rather than just sitting around theorizing about what may or may not happen. After all, to move through a dark room, it's better to take short, slow steps and learn from the bumps, especially if the alternatives are standing still and running.

Leaders can also institute changes through what I call **Innovation Incubators**. These are small creative teams tasked solely with experimentation. An example of how they work comes from my own life at Aptify. When I started Aptify in 1993, it was just me. A couple of years later I had a business partner and shortly after a handful of others joined our team. We knew nothing other than experimentation as we were creating a business from scratch. Over the years, as we achieved success and growth, we arrived at a point where we had so many people that I found it extremely hard to innovate. Even in a very innovative, entrepreneurial environment (in a software company that I had built no less), I felt that we had become incremental innovators and were not producing the big hits that put us on the map to begin with.

By that point in time, we were a global company with plenty of resources and engineers with brilliant minds, but as a team we weren't driving major change anymore. Instead, we were mostly thinking about how to improve what we had already built. We found ourselves in what Clayton Christenson famously dubbed "the innovator's dilemma," in his 1997 book of the same name, a common problem for successful businesses that we could not escape.

Over time, I arrived at the point where I decided that radical change was needed to inject meaningful innovation back into our organization. I created a completely separate team, called Innovation Laboratories, a group that would be forked off from the rest of the company, report directly to me, and include people who were brilliant with risk-oriented mind-sets. The goal was to have this team serve as an incubator for disruptive ideas. For this reason, I didn't give them the same accountability to produce day-to-day results as the rest of the team. Their mission was to think about long-term, highly disruptive change, and it worked amazingly well. Innovation Labs came up with all sorts of new ideas that had nothing to do with our current product, but that were significant innovations for the industry. Their success reenergized the company, and it gave our brand reputation a major industry boost.

WHO'S IN CHARGE? TACKLING VOLUNTEER LEADERSHIP TURNOVER AND HARNESSING STAFF POWER

The leadership structure of associations often operates more like a relay race than a marathon, with board members turning over about every eighteen to thirty-six months and president/chair tenures lasting one to two years, on average. Compared to most leadership structures in the for-profit sector—where board positions are often held for many more years and CEOs stay in command indefinitely, so long as board members, investors, and business goals are satisfied—associations are at a disadvantage when it comes to improving their culture.

For real change to happen and be seen all the way through, associations are depending on a rotation of short-term people to continue the same path, and drive toward the same goal. If you hand off to the next person and they don't want to pursue the same goal, then it gets lost, or they go a different direction. Now you're an organization that appears to be confused about who they are, why they're there, and what they want to be. Even worse is the fact that many association leaders remain wary of innovation, mostly because no one wants to be responsible for the failures of a noble cause. And who can blame them? Coupled with the uncertainty of who is in command and for how long, it's a prime recipe for either stagnation or directionless chaos.

Depending on the bylaws of the association, there isn't much that can be done to alter the length of tenure for board and executive positions. That isn't necessarily a bad thing, either. A rotating leadership structure can bring with it fresh ideas and attitudes that help reenergize the organization. But there's also a great potential for creating a choppy, discordant environment in which the big picture grows blurry and the staff resorts to focusing on shortsighted, individual tasks and goals instead.

It's another reason why having a strong sense of identity and purpose is so important to associations. If an organization has a clearly defined purpose and a well-designed culture firmly in place, then transitioning from one leader to another is a much smoother ordeal. A team sharing a collective purpose and set of values can adjust to new ideas and personalities with far less confusion and tension, not to mention fewer delays. The new leadership can set short and long-term objectives and introduce new ideas more easily, because they can measure them against the organization's purpose and values first. The presence of an engaged staff, meanwhile, will help ensure the completion of those objectives during the leadership's tenure. Put simply, your purpose and values, and the philosophy behind them, become anchoring points for leadership as they come in and out.

On the plus side, associations tend to retain their staff for long periods of time. In fact, it's rather common to tour associations and meet staff members who have been there for twenty years or more. At one association I visited recently, a staff member jokingly introduced himself as "the new guy," even though he had been with them for fifteen years. There's a hidden opportunity there, one that utilizes the stability of the staff to drive change. I say hidden, because the staff at most associations oftentimes think of themselves as subordinate to the board of directors. And they are, in terms of the hierarchy structure. They take their orders from the board, but the board's focus tends to be high-level. Even boards that are somewhat meddlesome in the day-to-day, which is not that common, are still focused more on the forest than the trees.

On the other hand, the staff is communicating with members, maintaining the association's online presence, producing the content, organizing meetings, and so on. As such, the staff controls most of the day-to-day power in an association. And day-to-day decision-making is really what drives either the reinforcement of a culture's foundation (i.e., values and purpose), or erodes it. The high-level issues occupying much of the leadership's time don't have as much of an impact. It's the small, daily wins and losses, along with the decisions and attitudes behind them that change what's going to actually happen in the future. A captain might see the shoreline on a map or through a scope, but it's the crew that ultimately decides whether it's possible to get there.

If you or someone else has a habit of saying, "I can't create any real change because I'm just the membership manager (or whatever position). I'm not the CEO. I'm not on the board. What can I do?" Well, the answer is *a lot*. The membership manager, for example, is in charge of the majority of the organization's communication with members. That gives them and anyone else in their department an incredible amount of influence over membership engagement, recruitment strategies, and the external representation of the organization's culture in general. No matter what position you may be in, identify what you have influence over first, and then think about how you can effect change through whatever influence your role affords. There is much more power in the day-to-day folks and the things they do, if they think about them the right way. It's the people on the ground who control the culture of an organization, the figurative sails of the ship.

SELLING YOUR PURPOSE

After I sold Aptify, I reinvested my energy into several other projects. Among them was rasa.io, a startup artificial intelligence company focused on helping associations curate the world's content and personalize it for each member. From my experience with Aptify, I knew the importance of defining a compelling Core Purpose early, so I initiated a discovery workshop at the company's onset. The point was to define a Core Purpose for our new company and establish it as a guiding light that could both inspire and instruct our ideology, our work, and the culture we built on top of it.

We had a small team during our early purpose discovery exercises, only about seven of us, which made the process much easier for many reasons. For one, it's just easier to really listen to a small, tightly knit group of people than it is to hear the ideas and beliefs of a large room full of people, many of whom probably don't know each other that well. For another, it made our hiring and onboarding process easier. We knew who we were, we knew who we were looking for, and in turn, so did our prospective teammates. We could be clear and upfront about who we were and what we cared about, as well as what we wanted from an individual on a more personal level. That allowed both sides to decide if we were a good fit earlier rather than later—a giant financial, emotional, and productivity benefit.

The goal of the exercise was to create a Core Purpose statement that qualified under the conditions that strive to be deeply and emotionally meaningful, something that would stand the test of time. Ultimately, the purpose statement we chose was, "To Better Inform the World." We chose that statement because we feel that a well-informed world increases the chances for so many good things to happen. It leads to better education, better professions, better opportunities to improve lives, a likelihood of a more peaceful future, and a host of other positive outcomes. For those reasons, it's a deeply meaningful and emotion-

---

Test how emotionally meaningful your Core Purpose is by asking a few simple questions first:

- If your organization were gone tomorrow, who would miss it? Put another way, does your "why" matter to anyone outside your immediate orbit?

- Ask people outside your organization, "What emotions do you feel when you hear our stated purpose? What does it mean to you?"

ally memorable purpose statement for us. Plus, it resonates with our client community as well, because associations also want to have an impact informing the world.

Interestingly, since choosing that Core Purpose statement, we have made better decisions toward reaching our goals than I think we would have without working with a strong purpose in mind. One example of that benefit came when we were developing our sales strategy.

rasa.io uses AI to produce personalized news briefs to people, which we send out every day or every week under the imagery of a particular brand. Our clients can optimize the briefs for several different scenarios, and then we can measure open rates, click-through rates, and many other statistics to determine if their efforts are being effective and offer insights into why or why not.

AI is a tool that someone could use for ethically questionable intentions, making the importance of our Core Purpose statement that much more critical. Every day, in every decision, we simply have to ask, "Are we better informing the world?" Maybe open rates (how many times a person actually opened the email) is the statistic that a potential advertiser wants to see, and maybe we can maximize the advertising revenue if we focus there. The problem is that if you make your news-letter an advertising vehicle and you overdo it, it really detracts from the value of the content. In a piece of content riddled with advertising, readers are no longer reading a clean, informative, easy-to-understand news brief. They are reading something that's clobbered with advertising, spurring doubts about the quality and credibility of not only the content, but the organization behind it as well.

This isn't to say open rates are a poor measure for the quality of the information we are sending. If open rates are consistently good, it usually means we are indeed on track in sending users content they find valuable. To build on this, however, we find that click rates are even more insightful. The click-through rate tells us that the person who opened the email found the content interesting enough to read more of it. Even though a potential advertiser is often more interested in open rates, we think the click-through rates are just as important, and in some cases, more important.

We made the decision not to include advertising for some time while we perfected the quality of the content our AI sends out to each individual. This is a hard decision to make, as adding ad revenue into the mix for our clients and us is something we could easily implement and derive significant financial benefit from. As we go forward, and make decisions on how much advertising to include, our primary goal is to make sure that we're upholding our central push, which is to make sure that every product we introduce is in alignment with our Core Purpose statement. In doing so, we are building a superior product through better outcomes for the end user, and better client relationships, all by proving to ourselves and others that we're serious about our purpose.

When the General Data Protection Regulation (GDPR) became a major topic of discussion in late 2017 and early 2018, we were a step ahead because we had decided early on that data privacy, and the right of an individual to control their data, was of critical importance in actually achieving our purpose statement. One can't claim to truly be seeking to better inform the world if they don't maintain the privacy of their users at the core of their operation. For us, when the European Union adopted the GDPR in 2016, it was very natural to embrace and we've gone far beyond the regulation because we know it's the right thing to do. Everyone who works for and with us knows this as well, in part because of our clear purpose statement.

Most organizations think of their marketing and sales strategy in a very simplistic frame of mind, such as the deceptively shallow importance of open rates in digital content. For many associations, marketing is just a process of getting members and then finding a way to keep them. Seems easy enough, right? Get a member, keep a member. Obviously there's more to it in reality, but if you think about the base sales model of the average association—member-centric comes to mind—most of what they do revolves around the idea of capturing members and then keeping them inside.

The problem with that is a lot of people today want a more casual relationship with a brand initially. I'll give you an example. Paid membership is an excellent business model to engage with an audience. I'm sure no one would argue that Amazon hasn't proven that argument in recent years. But what distinguishes Amazon from other membership-driven retailers is that you don't have to be a Prime member to transact business with Amazon. You don't even have to have an account to browse Amazon. If you want to buy something, you can check out with a very minimal amount of information and a low-friction purchasing process. Even if you've never been to the Amazon.com website, you can go buy paper clips or whatever other product you want and have it shipped to you in a matter of a couple minutes, a couple clicks. Amazon offers a simple, convenient, and autonomous environment that people today especially crave.

Amazon's brilliance is that they funnel users into an increasing level of engagement. One way they do that is with their Prime membership. For around a hundred bucks a year, you get a slew of benefits ranging from streaming television and movies to retail discounts, free shipping, and more. If you buy anything from Amazon on any basis that's reasonably frequent, then the Prime membership pays for itself. In fact, it actually makes more financial sense to become a member than it does not to, a phenomenon driven mostly by the shipping fees. Amazon bundled in free video and other benefits into the membership, effectively serving as the cherry on top for an already better deal. At the same time, Amazon does something other membership-driven retailers don't. They don't go to the world and say, "You must be a member to start doing business with us."

> *Associations often think that selling a membership is the first thing you do with someone. Doing it later is a key strategy to embrace in today's marketplace. Don't try to sell someone on the benefits of joining too aggressively. Rather, let the process go naturally and the benefits will sell memberships themselves.*

Most associations present their pricing structure to the public in terms of member versus non-member value. The member value is typically much better, and, of course, that isn't necessarily a bad thing. But structuring your business around the idea of getting people to become a member first is not as effective today as it was in years past. Today's membership consumers desire a more casual relationship, meaning associations—much like Amazon—are better off engaging with a broader audience earlier on and letting memberships sell themselves down the road. This is a large part of what the Open Garden Model is all about: letting people *into* the organization so they can better see the value of the organization's work and how members contribute outside its borders firsthand. Some people may choose to become members because of their experience, and others may never become members. Either way, a larger audience will have greater revenue potential and impact on achieving the organization's Core Purpose. The key is to create an experience that non-members value, and then building membership pricing around it. The added benefits of membership can then serve as purchase incentives, but often the intangible benefit of wanting to belong will cause people to join after they've gained more insight into and respect for the organization as a non-member.

Unfortunately, one of the biggest barriers associations have is that their business model isn't robust enough to casually engage with non-members. That creates a big problem for recruitment, because the people who want a quick, agile, easy interaction don't feel welcome by virtue of the design of the business. People may get that feeling from the design of the association's website, such as a lack of non-member content or frequent requests (even demands) for money and a commitment. Everything outward-facing that an association does, like its website, often stems from the overall thinking around member and non-member engagement. If all you do all day is think about how to get people to become members, when someone comes to you who isn't a member and doesn't want to be, you don't really know how to interact with them. The key there is to know how members want you to interact with them and to be able to adjust your approach individually.

Most associations understand that the structure of the organization centers on volunteers, followed by members. What many associations fail to see, however, is the potential financial benefits of including three other key groups in their marketing and events planning strategies:

1.   People who are interested in or contribute to the association's work but are not interested in memberships.

2.   People who are part of a related field but don't align with joining the association as a member.

3.   The general public, who are not likely to become members, but may be interested in resources the association can provide.

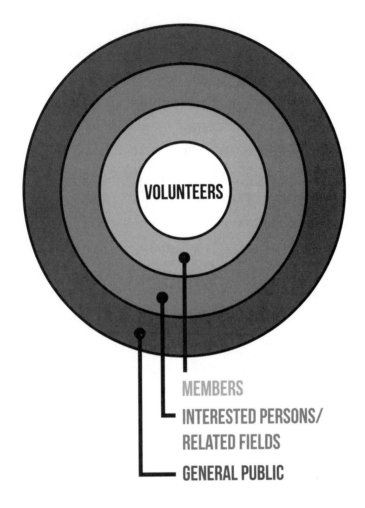

MEMBERS
INTERESTED PERSONS/
RELATED FIELDS
GENERAL PUBLIC

If you're not tuned into the entire structure of getting people to do something simple with you, they're far less likely to do anything with you.

Let's take the American Dental Association (ADA) as an example. If you were to ask the CEO of the ADA what the purpose of the American Dental Association is, she would tell you it is to improve oral health globally. Their purpose isn't to help dentists specifically, or to help member dentists be more successful. They do those things, but their purpose, ultimately, is to improve oral health around the world.

Now, if you asked a random staffer what their purpose is at any organization, you may not get the same answer. Certainly, if you asked several members of a random association what its purpose is, you're unlikely to get the same answer each time. Therein lies the challenge. The leadership at the American Dental Association very much believes in its purpose, and they plan accordingly to align with it. But the challenge is that the members who are funding the association typically think the association's mission is to advance the professional success of their members, improve the quality of care in our practice, and so on. Members rarely think of the association's larger purpose as a mission statement, if they think about it at all.

But if you ask the association leaders why helping members matters (usually you have to ask "why" several times to peel the layers back to Core Purpose), they will likely tell you that, by helping their members be more successful in their jobs, they are advancing their Core Purpose, which in the ADA's case is improving oral health around the globe. Oral health is not necessarily emotionally charged for everybody. It's an important health topic that can actually improve general health on a large scale, so improving oral health is a very meaningful purpose to have, if it's conveyed properly. If I told you that the ADA existed to improve the success of dentists, dentists would probably care about that, but few others would. Your Core Purpose needs to be an emotionally meaningful idea to people who are both outside and inside your organization.

If you were to draw a concentric circle of closeness to the center of the organization, you would find that as you get farther and farther away from the center, you often find that Core Purpose doesn't radiate outward in a consistent manner. That is a challenge and opportunity. I believe that if associations do a good job of expressing their Core Purpose on a daily basis, live that purpose, and communicate it consistently, then their decision-making will be in line with their Core Purpose much more so than if they relegate their purpose to a plaque in the boardroom (which oftentimes is the case, unfortunately). That's not the case with ADA. They do a good job of expressing their Core Purpose, but my point is that organizations have a bigger opportunity with Core Purpose than many realize. Purpose can really be a guiding beacon for organizations if they look at it the right way, focusing especially on how it can connect them to a larger audience and market.

That's why growth becomes a purpose issue, in the end. Your purpose doesn't just permeate everything your organization does internally; it lays the groundwork for how you communicate with the people inside and out of your organization, quietly setting the stage for what ultimately happens when you do engage with them. If you have a purpose that's all about getting people to enter the **walled garden**, which is membership models, then it becomes a lot harder to think of ways to engage people outside that wall. The purpose you assign to yourself or others is the same one that's inevitably given as the reason why people should join. In other words, it sets the tone for the relationship even before it begins. It sends subliminal messages through every interaction you have with your audience, i.e. website design, the association's media content, interpersonal communications with the staff, who you book for events. Purpose is alive 24/7/365. It is present at every point of contact an organization has with staff, members, and non-members. With that much presence and influence, your ability to hone in on the simplest, most inspiring, and thought-provoking North Star will determine your chances for successful growth more than anything else. It's the proverbial foundation of your organization's staff, leadership, member base, and content. In other words, without a purpose, there is nothing.

CHAPTER WORKSHOP

» How do you find your purpose?

- Ask yourself repeatedly why the organization exists. It usually takes five to seven times asking "why" before you arrive at a deeper, more emotionally charged answer.

- Recruit an expert to help your group discover its purpose. Doing so offers an outside perspective that challenges the assumptions that tend to develop in an echo chamber.

- "Where do you feel the most pride?" Answering this question provides direction during times of discouragement or confusion.

- "If we were gone tomorrow, who would miss us?" Answering this question helps you gain insight into what people outside of the organization value the most about you.

» To implement change, you will need to:

1. **Show vulnerability**. Don't present an image of infallibility. This leads to a fear of failure, which leads to risk aversion, and ultimately a lack of innovation.

2. **Experiment.** Carve out enough time and opportunities to experiment.

3. **Make progression projects a priority**. It's not financial constraints that make this time impossible. It's a deficiency in willingness.

4. **Diversify sources**. Expand your sources of information to avoid recirculating the same ideas. Eventually you will grow uninspired, which contributes to the fear of change. Get excited about what's possible, and the challenges will shrink.

5. **Start small**. Scale the scope of the problem down, rather than trying to cut it out all at once. Keep a small team of decision-makers in the innovation process. Let individuals make small changes to their own work.

SUGGESTED READING

Great by Choice by James C. Collins and Morten T. Hansen

Scaling Up: How a Few Companies Make It ... and Why the Rest Don't by Verne Harnish *The Innovator's Dilemma* by Clayton Christenson

Chapter Three

LEADING THROUGH VALUES

Values are like fingerprints. Nobody's are the same,
but you leave 'em all over everything you do.

—ELVIS PRESLEY

There are two parts toward establishing the culture of any organization. First, there is the **ideological** component (i.e., defining Core Purpose and Core Values), which you would be right to imagine as a process akin to the idea of soul searching. It's the journey to understand *why* you exist (Core Purpose) and *how* you should behave (Core Values) to support those conclusions in ways that are more philosophical than practical. The answers form the core ideology of an organization, a set of convictions that should inspire and direct its business strategies, managerial style, marketing campaigns, even the very products/services it designs and delivers to its customers.

Additionally, the ideology should guide what not to do just as much as what makes sense to do. Saying no to the wrong ideas is even more critical than saying yes to the right ones.

Once you have discovered and agreed upon those philosophical elements, you must then prepare for the challenge of putting them into action. This is the **operational** component of the process which, as you might have guessed, never ends. Make no mistake; implementing these rather abstract ideas throughout your organization is a long and complicated process that must be done with regularity for the lifetime of the organization.

At first, putting these ideological elements into action almost feels as though someone has asked you to build furniture out of music—a strange demand to turn something intangible and emotional into something everyone can reach out, touch, and actually use every day. It's the interweaving of the ideological and the operational that's difficult. Meeting that demand is really a question of how successful you are at defining and implementing a set of **Core Values**, which are the set of behaviors that an organization agrees to hold itself up to while pursuing its Core Purpose. Once put in place, Core Values should be immutable and at all times non-negotiable. Put another way, Core Values aren't to be ignored on rainy days—only applied and adhered to when convenient. Core Values have to be as solid as the foundational layer of Core Purpose they are built on top of.

The other challenge you'll run into, when going from ideology to operation, is that you'll be repeating yourself regularly. To some, this may become mundane and unnecessary. Regardless of how repetitive it may seem, getting an ideology well rooted in an organization is a long-term, eternal game that requires patience and the persistent reinforcement of opportunities to discuss Core Purpose and Core Values. In other words, you have to outlast folks that think you're just doing the latest initiative and show them you're serious by walking the talk and ensuring that everyone else does the same. It takes time, repetition, and above all else, a great deal of patience.

A LESSON IN DISCOVERY: ORIGINS OF VALUES AND HOW TO FIND THEM

I like to use the expression "discovering your values," as opposed to defining them. Jim Collins talks about the importance of making that distinction as well; I think that values are already ingrained into people. Whether through their upbringing, education, childhood environment, or other experiences and influences they encountered in their early life, individual values already exist. But, over time, they may be buried in the subconscious.

Once they enter adulthood, every individual has their own personal Core Values, which set the standard for one's behavior, and form their perception of what is important in their life. The Core Values for an individual don't change very much over time after early adulthood, which isn't necessarily a bad thing. One would hope that people believe in a particular set of underlying values, things like honesty, decency, work ethic, and trustworthiness. Those are the obvious ones that most people try to adhere to. Would you want to interact with anybody who doesn't uphold these common values?

While everyone has a specific set of values, they are rarely asked to identify them. However, what happens in a discovery session is that a group of individuals come together and creates a set of values that uniquely define what is different and compelling about their organization. At times, that means rarely discussed values will suddenly come into glaring focus. The effect can be intimidating and intense, but everyone should be heard and have his or her values considered, without exception. That doesn't mean that an organization's Core Values should be settled upon through some kind of a formula where you collect the Core Values of the individuals and group them together to find the most common ones. Core Values may be settled upon that way, but values are most interesting, authentic, and effective when you adhere to a deeper, more meaningful discovery process to find them.

For the individuals involved, that process begins by looking at the behavior you demand from everyone, versus the behavior you absolutely will not tolerate from anyone. Keep in mind that both are very important to think about regularly. Like Core Purpose, you don't discover Core Values through some theoretical practice, such as placing a plaque in the boardroom that says, "Our Core Values are X, Y, and Z." I'm not saying you don't put them on the wall; that's one of the many things you should do to keep your values alive. I mean that your Core Values should be something that, like your purpose, you build into your day-to-day decision-making.

Let's be clear here. You have to bring your purpose to life every day. Values are different. Values don't help you live your purpose. Values are how you behave, while purpose is why you exist. These are very different concepts, and they don't necessarily tie into each other the way one might think they do. That doesn't mean that values should determine right from wrong. If the values picked for an organization are the fundamental kind, such as integrity and courage, then you will probably have trouble getting people to remember them, much less believe in them. You may also find yourself saying, "This person doesn't have x value, so they're a bad person." Obviously, that's a questionable leadership tactic. If you're measuring performance based on vague character traits and trying to judge individuals for attributes that are often difficult to assess, then you don't have the right Core Values as an organization. Core Values should be differentiating between organizations, rather than the obvious, more generic ones that do little to inspire or inform your team's behavior.

I pick on commonly held values like honesty and integrity all the time, because, to me, there's no point in talking about them. Those are get-in-the-game values, the kind that shouldn't have to be said. Does anyone not value integrity, trustworthiness, work ethic, courage, or success? Look at Enron. One of their Core Values was "Integrity" and it didn't play out quite that way. It isn't the fact that they declared Integrity, of course, that caused their deep-rooted problems. However, the fact that their values were generic certainly meant they weren't really part of the conversation on a daily basis. Without those decency values, no one will want to do anything with you anyway, so focus on values that give you a distinct identity instead. If your values are generic, then they

Enron's Core Values

- Integrity

- Communication

- Respect

- Excellence

mean nothing. In fact, it's worse than not having them at all, because they will appear insincere and unoriginal, ultimately becoming a joke over time.

I'll give you an example of a value that's a little different from those types of empty values. One of the Core Values at rasa.io is "Simpler is Better." Simplicity as a core value? Yes. We don't mean that our products are simple. We mean that we value simplicity, and when we can find a way to make the ideological functional but less complex, we pursue it. The way we think about decision-making— how we build our product, how we price it, or how we interact with a customer in a customer service inquiry—revolves around the value of simplicity. We want to find a way to make it simpler every time, because it's better for the customer, and for us. That's the key to discovering Core Values: settling on the behaviors and attitudes that are best for the organization and all those it interacts with. This particular value is one I personally align with deeply. At Aptify, we created powerful software, but it was often very complex and required extensive training. From this experience, I decided that at rasa.io, I wanted our values to directly instruct our decision-making every day. Forging simplicity into our values ensures that "easy to use" overrides "sophisticated" every time. Although, funnily enough, a simpler solution usually requires a far more sophisticated technical approach.

An organization really needs to be able to answer the *why*, *where*, and *how* of their culture. Their Core Purpose answers why the organization exists; their vision answers where it wants to end up; their Core Values are in place to answer how they will get there. However, there's more than one way to achieve the same outcome—the way one organization goes about it can be very different from another, and it can even change as the organization evolves. Nevertheless, values shape and guide what you do on the ground day-to-day and how your team behaves with one another. If you say that you value simplicity, then it becomes a guiding force for many decisions you make. That doesn't mean that simplicity is placed above all else, but it becomes an important value that everyone knows, supports, and can use as a measuring stick when making daily decisions on their own.

How do you discover your values? The process will be a little different for everyone, as it depends to some degree on the size and purpose of the organization and the types of exercises in which you choose to partake. I can tell you that our experience at rasa.io was a typical Core Values discovery exercise.

Every team member took the time to sit in a room together and discuss how we felt about the work that each of us did. We talked about our personal values, and the ones we felt were the most important for us to focus on as an organization. Then we built a list of values we felt best described the right candidate to hire. It began as a long list, comprised of some fifteen to twenty candidate values. From that list, we whittled them down by grouping them together based on their similarities in concept and eliminated any redundancies. We worked to wordsmith the language until it felt right for our team. For us, the way we express our values is as critical as the name of the value itself. What we ended up with is a clear way of understanding how these values actually need to be lived.

RASA.IO CORE VALUES

Demand Diversity in Thought

We demand all of our team members seek out ideas beyond their own. Diverse ideas often come from diverse people and sources. Be creative and seek to turn over stones and coax out ideas from people who may not always be first to share them.

Simpler Is Better

Find the simplest possible way to solve each problem. Unnecessary steps, features, or processes must be cut with extreme discipline.

Tell It Like It Is

No matter what, say what you mean and mean what you say. Do this while practicing empathetic listening.

Learn by Doing

We are not afraid to start things with little information or insight, experiment, fail, iterate and try again. We strive to find the best way to solve hard problems with a bias towards action. We work hard to share our learning along the way so that we can get better as individuals and as a team through this process.

Measure It

If you can't measure it, you can improve it. Measure everything that you are shooting for and tell it like it is along the way.

Own It

As a team and as individuals we own our individual outcomes end to end. When we sign up for something, we get it done. As a team there is no "they" there is only "us" and "we" and we all own our success together. We vigorously debate our goals, once we set them, even if we didn't all agree, we all own them together.

Celebrate Success

Celebrating success means celebrating both the success and the steps that lead to success including embracing the failures along the way and the need to start from a position of inexperience.

At rasa.io, we had the advantage of holding our discovery sessions while we were still small and compact. You may be part of a much larger and well-established organization and be asking yourself, "Who gets to come into that conversation to discover the values of the organization?" I found myself in the same situation at Aptify, where we didn't begin the discovery process until many years after I founded the company. At the time, we had more than one hundred employees, so we obviously couldn't bring everyone in to discuss their values in great detail the way we did at rasa.io. If that's the case for you, then you may want to follow Jim Collins's advice, and use what he calls "The Mars Group," which comprises people who have been elected to serve as ambassadors or representatives for various groups of team members during the discovery process.

Aptify used our executive leadership team, which represented all corners of the organization, for the discussion. However, if I had to do it over again, I wouldn't just take the top people. I would include a handful of people that are in the core leadership team, but I would also pick a few people from the lower ranks as well to ensure that we had a more diverse set of thoughts. Instead, we used the leadership team to represent each department during the discovery process, which still generated great results, because we were fortunate to have leaders in place that knew their teams and did a great job of speaking on their behalf.

Just know that whoever is involved in your Core Values discovery sessions will ultimately have a hand in deciding how everyone within the organization behaves and the decisions they make on a daily basis. Choose your role models wisely, but keep in mind that it's sometimes the last ones you would think of who contribute the most to the process. Diversity of thought and an open, supportive environment are critical in this exercise, as they ensure that the results are multi-dimensional, useful, and unique to your organization.

ARE YOUR VALUES WORKING?

We know that the ideas behind organizational culture must go beyond theory if they are to be useful to the organization. It doesn't matter how good a player is, they won't help the team win by sitting on the sidelines—the same thing with values. The value set that the discovery team created should be communicated at every meeting, project directive, team-building exercise, and any other chance a leader has to remind his or her team, to ensure they are woven into the very fabric of the organization.

An organization's values are alive and working when they are second nature to its team members. One should be able to walk around the workspace not as a leader, but as an observer, and hear people talking about their values in any discussion. Whether it's during a product planning meeting or a sales huddle, people should be talking about purpose and values, especially if they're talking about decision-making. If someone says, "Hey, we've got this project, but we're not sure about this idea for it," the conversation should always include, "Does it support our Core Purpose? Is it aligned with our Core Values?" Those concepts are the pulse of any organization, so if you spend a day running around the organization and don't hear people talking about purpose and values, then you have more work to do.

More often than not, values are forgotten. Core Values, while they may be refined in their interpretation over time, should remain a constant in the culture of an organization. The fact that their disappearance is not part of the conversation at all is a big problem. People will tell you they have a clear purpose and set of values. But if that's the case, then everyone in the organization should be able to tell you what they are without having a printout in front of them. In associations especially, staff will generally give you one answer with respect to their mission: "We're here to serve our members." Likewise, if you ask a member of the association why it's there, they are likely to tell you that the association is there to help its members. That's not a bad explanation, but it's a shortsighted and narrow perspective of the association's purpose and contributions that lends evidence to the view of an association not living up to its fullest potential.

The very term "purpose statement" is a foreign concept to many associations. Most of them have mission statements, but mission statements sometimes are problematic to an organization finding its purpose and values. A mission statement combines the why and how, and sometimes it will include a piece about where you want to end up. You can think of it as if the mission and the vision were blurred together in a way that is unnecessarily voluminous and vague as compared to a purpose statement. Having so many indistinct and uninspired reasons for why one exists results in the association market being under-served by the culture ideology, as they don't really get to the heart of their work. Serving members is what they do, but it's not necessarily why they're there. And why they are there is what makes associations special. Their purpose is often what sets them apart from others in a way that is very attractive to the average person, whether they're active in the association's field of interest or not.

I revisit purpose only to say that a meaningful purpose statement helps set the stage to revisit our values as an organization. Most of us, whether as an individual or an organization, have a set of values defined, but when was the last time you revisited and perhaps refreshed your values? Your values may be fine, but in some cases a person or organization's values are defined in such generic ways that they sound and feel meaningless. Let me give you an example of that.

When we set out to define our Core Values at rasa.io, rather than using the word "accountability," we used the phrase "own it." At

Aptify, "Accountable" was one of our four Core Values. At rasa.io, we wanted to use more action-oriented vocabulary when defining our values. For us, "own it" made sense, because the meaning seemed more obvious. It was like saying, "Hey, if you take something on, you own it. You take it to the end and make sure it gets done well, because you will be held responsible for the outcome." The vernacular was commonplace and well understood by our team, while the meaning was clearly stated with a direct tone—all of which satisfied the style and goals we wanted as a group for our value demands.

> *The vernacular was commonplace and well understood by our team, while the meaning was clearly stated with a direct tone—all of which satisfied the style and goals we wanted as a group for our value demands.*

Sometimes a shift like that in your values makes a lot of sense. A good friend of mine, Tom Turner, ran a company in Nashville, called DSi, before selling it just a few months before writing this book. One of the Core Values Tom put in place at DSi was called "Win the Right Way," which tells you a lot. There are many ways that people express the same idea, but "Win the Right Way" tells a story. It lets you know in a very concise and memorable way that DSi values success, hard work, and good ethics. Core Values like the one Tom presented to his team tend to be remembered by both clients and staff. And as a result, they have a greater impact on how people behave. Tom took the ideas behind his Core Values and found unique ways to live them on a daily basis. As an example, he named each of his conference rooms after a core value, so instead of meeting in "Conference Room B," you would meet in the "Win The Right Way" conference room. Simple and effective ways of constantly reminding team members of Core Values are critical to making them come alive in the culture.

VALUE MEMBERS: HOW VALUES DETERMINE WHO'S IN, WHO'S OUT

A unique challenge for association leaders is the prospect of balancing organizational values with the values of people over which they have little control. An association largely depends on members and volunteers, two groups whose alignment with organizational values can be difficult to assess and maintain. It may feel counterintuitive, but instilling somewhat polarizing values is an effective way to ensure that an association finds a committed staff and member base that are with them to the end. No organization is a great fit for everyone, and if leaders figure that out on the front end, the organization will be much stronger as it pushes forward.

You should be willing to hire and fire based on values. You should be willing to recruit and retain members based on your purpose, but you can also use your values to measure alignment between external appeal and internal ideals. When out of sync, you know that your values are either not being lived inside the organization or they are simply not translating to those outside of it. If you have a "tell like it is" value in your system, for example, and you have someone in your organization who's not telling it like it is, even if they are otherwise performing in their job, then you have to find a way to coach them up, or ultimately get them out of your organization. It's really hard to change a person's value system, and if they're not capable of buying into the organization's Core Values, then everyone inside and outside the organization will question the importance of and commitment to its values.

We started by hiring people who understood and exhibited our Core Values. This allowed everyone involved to know what would be expected of them. Anyone that didn't feel our values matched their own was free to go. The next thing we had to figure out was how we would communicate these new values to existing staff. It was great if we could get the culture aligned through the hiring pipeline, but how could we communicate what was going on to everyone else?

One way to gauge whether a person is a good cultural fit is by using a values-productivity graph. One axis measures a person's output, which is productivity skills combined with effort level, and the other measures a person's alignment with values. In the top right corner you have your "A players," people who are highly productive and highly aligned with values. These are the people who both fit your culture and are doing great work. If you go down one box in the right-hand quadrant, you have people who are highly productive, but are low in values alignment. Those people are dangerous, because they're outputting work, they're selling product, they're writing code, or whatever they're doing in their job, but they're toxic to your culture. In the top-left corner of graph are the people who are low in productivity but high in values alignment. They're a problem as well, but they're not as toxic as those who are culturally misaligned. Those people, also known as "B players," you can invest in through education and training. Assuming they have the raw intellect and the willingness needed, they can train for almost any skill so long as the person has the desire, intelligence, and adequate alignment of values. The people in the bottom-left corner, however, are the worst players in the company, because they're low in both productivity and values alignment. You must get rid of them quickly, as they are toxic to your culture and a drain on productivity.

Where many managers fail is with those in the bottom-right box. Leadership often overlooks or excuses workers who are high in productivity but low in values, because they are top producers. The problem is that this group, more than any other, kills your culture by sending a message that the organization does not actually believe in its values. Rather, it prioritizes short-term productivity and profit over the way its people behave.

At rasa.io, we started hiring people who understood and exhibited our Core Values. By doing so, the expectations of every person involved in our company were clear, from applicants and new hires to our existing staff to the leadership team. Anyone who doesn't feel our values match their own is free to go. In fact, we encourage and help anyone to find a path toward the future they desire, whether it's within our company or not. The last thing you want in a team member is someone who doesn't want to be in the organization, much less believe in it. Every organization has those people within their ranks at some point. Most of the time they stay there because they don't know where else to go, or because they don't realize they're misaligned with the organization's culture, which never made its values and purpose clear.

By failing to make good on your commitment to values, you're not just putting your culture at risk, you're putting your entire organization in jeopardy. In his book *Awesomely Simple*, John Spence, a well-respected author and friend of mine tells the story of a high-producing Fortune 500 executive. John was consulting for a large corporation in New York City when he learned of the problems they were having with one of their top producing execs. The individual was one of the firm's best performers, generating millions of dollars in profit for the firm every year. The problem was that he was an absolute nightmare to work with, and, by all accounts, just a terrible person in general. He was so misaligned with the firm's Core Values that he was not only disrupting the productivity of his colleagues, but diminishing their belief in them as well.

The leadership team asked John what they should do, and he responded by showing them a chart similar to the one I outlined on the previous page. John explained that the person had low values alignment, mixed with very high productivity, and why that is toxic to an organization's culture. "It's not even a question; you need to get rid of this person," John told them. They ultimately did decide to get rid of someone: John. They stopped using him as a consultant immediately. Though there were many other problems within the firm's culture, it fell apart shortly after they dismissed John's services. This one massive corporation is out of business now, and I believe it's largely due to the fact that they valued near-term results over creating a healthy culture.

The Open Garden Model really starts to be meaningful when a strong Core Purpose statement and Core Values statement are able to connect everyone. Your purpose and values should align the full-time employees, those who volunteer, and those who elect to join your organization because they believe in what the organization believes. You will find your strongest member base in those who join because they're moved by your purpose and values, not just because a nice package of benefits is involved. The latter is purely an economic decision, and because it's not an emotional decision, you will not get the same amount of loyalty, participation, and overall contribution from your members. The minute they think they can get a better deal somewhere else, those bargain-shoppers will leave. However, if one joins because they share the same values and big-picture purpose as the organization, they will most likely stay a member for as long as they believe the organization is committed to those ideals. In addition, non-members will also find emotional alignment with the core ideology (purpose + values) and that in turn will result in more meaningful and longer lasting relationships.

CHAPTER WORKSHOP

» On a daily basis, what are you doing to live your Core Values?

» How do you know that your Core Values are alive in your organization?

» If your Core Values don't form the heartbeat of your organization, you first need to make sure you're communicating them clearly and regularly. Write your Core Values on the wall, include them in newsletters, put them on your website, ask team members to recite them as often as necessary (one-on-one reviews, in the halls, at team-building events, etc.)

  □ Even once your Core Values have been discovered and sufficiently communicated inside the organization, don't declare victory and then go to sleep at the wheel. You need to keep going. For thirty seconds at the beginning of every meeting, you should read one of your Core Values. Make it clear by stating, "This is a core value." In the beginning, it's going to feel very strange for people, but it will get easier and the weirdness will dissipate from the room a little more each time a leader states one of the Core Values in the meeting.

  □ During these staff meetings, highlight examples of Core Values being lived out by members of the team. In a typical team at Aptify, the leader of the meeting would call out someone who had lived a core value that particular week. For instance, they might say, "Hey, Alicia, we really appreciate the fact that you 'owned it' when this particular customer called. You didn't know how to answer their question, but rather than passing them off to somebody else, you stayed with them from the problem to the finish line. Your actions were highly responsive, and because you owned it end-to-end, you ultimately solved their problem." It takes very little time and energy to recognize a team member following through on the organization's values, and yet such a recognition motivates the whole team by reinforcing the importance of and gratitude for the organization's commitment to values.

» Encourage Core Values at the peer-to-peer level. Leaders have to set the tone in any organization. One way is to have tools available that encourage each value through Core Value cards. Take the time to create "value postcards." On the front of the card, use an interesting photograph or graphic that illustrates a particular Core Value as well as a written description of it. On the back of the card, leave space for a team member to write a note expressing their appreciation for another team member's commitment to a specific Core Value. The exercise helps team members visualize organizational values, but it also offers a way for people to quickly and easily communicate or receive gratitude and encouragement without the necessity of a meeting or special event.

- Display **Core Values posters** in meeting rooms and ask team members to open each meeting by reading one of the Core Values and its description.

- **Employee Recognition.** Distribute cards of each value for employees to give each other with hand written notes to recognize a coworker living a specific value.

SUGGESTED READING

Turn the Ship Around by David Marquet

Awesomely Simple by John Spence

SECTION II
THE SOIL

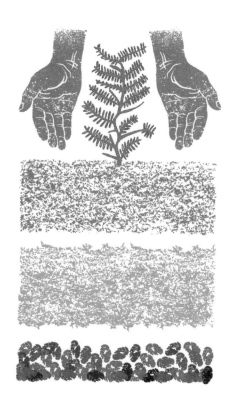

Chapter Four

ASSESSING THE LANDSCAPE

We have two ears and one mouth, so we
should listen more than we say.

—ZENO OF CITIUM

At Aptify, I spent a lot of time asking my team for feedback. Without notice, I would go to people individually and have casual one-on-ones with them. "Tell me what you're thinking," I would say. "How are you feeling about this current project we're working on?" I wouldn't say, "How's it going in general?" I named the project and them something specifically related to it. "The X project. What do you think about this component of it?" I would ask, and then I would wait patiently for them to respond. Every time I conducted these one-on-ones, I got more out of my team members than most of the other feedback methods I tried (cards, apps, email surveys, etc.).

That was important to me, because without having a firm grasp on what was happening in and around the company and how people felt about it, I knew I couldn't make decisions that moved the company forward without jarring my team, my clients, or myself too much in the process. An organization must move as a single unit, and it must also be aware of the impact its movements will have on those around it. Your people (staff, volunteers, members, and those with an interest or potential interest in the association) hold the intel that's necessary for such gliding movements.

Changes in culture also span the inside and the outside of an organization, making feedback a necessary component to understanding the effects of those changes. Failure to keep a pulse on those effects allows any damages, should something go off track, to grow deep and irreversible. Ideally, you want to know how people perceive your organization before you make any changes to its foundation (i.e., its Core Purpose and Core Values). Feedback is essential to measuring the general mood of your staff, members, and even the general public. However, the quality of your feedback very much depends upon the tone the organization's leadership sets beforehand. How well a leadership team listens to its people—both inside and outside the organization—goes farther than you might imagine in determining what they say, how they express it, and how well leaders interpret it. Perhaps more important to obtaining reliable feedback, though, is the degree of regularity and transparency leaders use when expressing themselves.

In business, we sometimes harbor feelings that a leader is not supposed to be vulnerable. But a key to good leadership in the Open Garden Model is actually rooted in the complete opposite: you have to legitimately demonstrate vulnerability to your team to receive sincere and useful feedback. No matter how many different formats you provide for people to give feedback, if they don't believe you're interested in listening to them, no one is going to provide it. Some people may try, and those who do will either be brutally honest out of some long-held frustration, or they will censor their feedback for fear of retaliation. Most, however, will not waste their time.

You have to legitimately demonstrate vulnerability to your team to receive sincere and useful feedback.

The kind of leader who is reflective, insightful, and willing to listen is rare, and that has a lot to do with those traits requiring more practice than we often believe they do. Good, empathetic listening skills and patient, measured responses aren't qualities that come naturally to most people. Demonstrating vulnerability means you have to get in front of people and show that you're not an all-knowing person, which is a difficult and seemingly unnatural thing for leaders to do. Even so, good organizational assessments depend on reliable feedback, which can only come when people feel comfortable sharing it. It takes a lot of time and effort to build such an environment because you have to earn trust from individuals, not just your team as a whole.

At Aptify, I never stopped asking for feedback. I made sure I was very specific because I knew that general, vague questions would only produce general, vague answers, which are meaningless to the process of building trust. Once they started talking specifics, I knew I could get more out of them that I could use when trying to improve the project, their experience, my leadership abilities, and the company as a whole.

Again, it's in your tone that you demonstrate vulnerability. By taking feedback and acting upon it, people will believe that taking the risk (and providing feedback is perceived as a risk) will be worth it, because something positive might actually come from it. If you don't agree with the feedback, be clear about why not to avoid creating a black hole that people's efforts disappear into. Over a long period, this will build a robust feedback loop, enabling better decision-making and a more connected and collaborative environment once you do.

After you set an open and receptive tone, there are multiple ways to actually obtain the feedback. Perhaps the most common is the old-fashioned **employee survey**. It's a little overhead-intensive, so I suggest doing them only once or twice a year, and making them as detailed as you feel is necessary to gain a solid understanding of your current employee population and the mind-sets within it. You may have your HR department conduct these surveys, but most organizations today prefer using a third-party tool to help assure team members that their answers will be kept anonymous.

The same strategy should be used when seeking feedback from the outside in. You're multiplying the tactic out to people that you're not as connected with, e.g. your members, constituents, the customers, whoever these external folks may be. To obtain quality feedback from them, you have to have the tools and capabilities to get feedback in, of course, but you also have to demonstrate that you're interested in the feedback of your external community as well.

The worse your culture is, the worse your feedback is going to be. To avoid that problem, many organizations have preferred sticking their figurative heads in the sand, and ignoring any feelings of discontent, frustration, or apathy from their respective internal and external communities. With websites and apps like Glassdoor, LinkedIn, Google reviews, Foursquare, Yelp, and many others allowing individuals to rate their experience, it's increasingly important to set a healthy tone to get sincere feedback before problems fester and grow into the kind that you cannot easily resolve.

Be ready for complaints. In fact, when you first ask for feedback, you're probably going to get a laundry list of complaints. As a leader, you may feel that some of them are totally unfair and unreasonable. If you react to them swiftly and negatively, however, then you're basically telling the individual that you did not expect good information from them anyway. You have to take time to work through their feedback carefully and thoughtfully in order to avoid sending the message that you don't respect their ideas and feelings.

I mentioned the job review site Glassdoor, which is an interesting tool for crowdsourcing feedback from people about a particular organization or CEO. It's also an easy way for people who are unhappy to flame a company anonymously. They don't have to say who they are, nor do they have to prove that they are, or ever were, really part of the company in question. Managers can also ask their team members to go on and provide positive feedback for the organization, so perhaps the reliability of the feedback is suspect on both sides of the equation.

Nonetheless, Glassdoor hosts a wealth of information that helps illustrate how people are generally experiencing a specific organization. When I was running Aptify, I looked at Glassdoor regularly and personally responded to every review about Aptify. If there were any complaints, I would respond with something along the lines of, "What you're saying here I understand. This is why we did x, or this is why we didn't do x." If the feedback was something generic or nonspecific, I would respond by saying, "Can you add some more detail here? What you're providing is interesting for us to understand, because it's clearly a concern to you and we're sorry you're not having a great experience." If they were a former employee that didn't have a good experience, I would tell them that we would like to get more information from them to ensure that others don't have the same experience. I always ended my responses with, "Here's my number." I then posted my personal cellphone number in the message. "Call me anytime if you want to talk about this, or email me, because I'd love to hear your thoughts in more detail."

That didn't mean I agreed with the reviews. Some of the reviews would say things that I thought were unfair. But what we found was that, by virtue of the CEO taking the time to write these responses and making themselves available on a personal level, we could establish an atmosphere that encouraged productive dialogue and conflict resolution. The way a leader handles a complaint or problem might actually convert the person or others into your most loyal customers, members, employees, clients, or advocates.

For some organizations, it may make more sense to conduct **group** or **one-on-one feedback sessions**, in which leaders and workers get together on a regular basis to discuss the pros and cons of their position, projects, and general work experience. These can be intimidating and uncomfortable at first, so I suggest bringing in an outside facilitator to help initiate and moderate the sessions.

For Aptify, I had the benefit of an expert facilitator from a company called Petra Coach (www.petracoach.com). There are many excellent coaches and facilitators available to help with this type of process. They will also instruct everyone involved on how to get the most from these conversations, as an individual and as a team. You may be asked to reveal what you like or dislike about a teammate's work, as well as what you believe your own strengths and weaknesses are and how they contribute to the overall performance of those around you.

Again, this is an exercise that can stir emotions in ways that may not be productive if executed in the wrong way, so having a knowledgeable consultant present is the wisest option when kickstarting the process. On the plus side, sitting down face-to-face with your team, or individual members of your team, and verbally expressing your feedback respectfully, with the idea in mind of helping yourself and others improve, is one of the best ways to nurture an open, collaborative, and expressive culture in your organization.

Many leaders will say, "I ask for feedback all the time, but I don't receive any. I guess everything is fine." In the context of culture assessment, no news is not good news. If an organization's leadership solicits feedback by sending out an email once a quarter saying, "Please give us your feedback. We'd like to hear from you." Clearly those organizations are not going to get good feedback. And they may wonder why, despite the fact that they are not doing the work. Others may turn to surveillance techniques. Whether it's an "undercover boss" strategy, or other methods to passively gain feedback, it's unnecessary and will likely create a lack of trust in the environment. That doesn't mean that in certain organizations it doesn't make sense to have people test your service and make sure the quality is there, but the kind of culture that's purposeful, transparent, and has real leadership is founded on a demonstrable desire to help people grow. That is the only way you will earn people's trust and gain consistently useful feedback, which enables dependable assessments of an organization's internal culture and external climate.

REMOVING THE ROT TO STIMULATE GROWTH

Trust is not just beneficial to quality feedback. In environments where trust is lacking, everyone pays an incredible emotional tax every day that dramatically reduces the probability of a fulfilled existence within the organization.

Frankly, if you run into a situation during a period of cultural reform where certain people (particularly those in management and leadership roles) are not prioritizing trust among their teams, you may have to make some tough choices about restructuring your team. I'm not telling you to go through and fire anyone who doesn't immediately agree with the changes. That's obviously harsh and would probably result in the firing of most people in the organization, considering there will likely be plenty of resistance to these types of changes in the beginning. Over time, you will realize who really doesn't want to be part of the organization's new direction. Once you do, you must sit down with that person and talk openly with them to assess the reasoning behind their resistance, looking for ways you may be able to help them resolve whatever conflicts they are having. In my own experience, I always aim for a direct, but understanding approach. "Look, I'm really getting a lot of resistance from you on this," I say. "I'm not asking you to agree with everything I'm saying. What I'm asking you to do is to participate fully. I don't feel you're doing that. I feel that you're resisting participation, that you're not on the bus in terms of where we're going. Is that true?"

If you have that kind of honest conversation with them, either the person will very rapidly "get on the bus," or they will choose to leave and you can help them with that decision. If you fail to do that, the rest of the team will sink. In a team of fifty, it only takes two or three negative voices to poison the whole team. Even if they were once a great asset to the company—and maybe in terms of their output they still are—if their attitude isn't aligned with the organization's Core Values and where it's trying to go, it's better for the individual, their team, and the organization to remove them. Instead, help them find a future career path that is aligned with their views and goals, which isn't where they currently are.

"Freeing up the future of an individual," as it's sometimes called, is a really important part of an organization's cultural rebooting process. No organization hires 100 percent perfectly. In fact, on average, most organizations have less than a 50 percent success rate on hiring. Yet, voluntary attrition in most nonprofits is very low, partly because people typically are not fired or pushed out. The people who are quitting are usually the ones going on to opportunities they find to be better.

It isn't enough to get rid of the bad apples, either. You aren't reorganizing your team and replacing someone because they're a bad person. You're replacing team members, and sometimes volunteers or even members, because they're a bad fit for the organization. Most leaders will kick the can down the road for as long as they possibly can when it comes to personnel changes. When I ask leaders why they hesitate for so long, the most common response is, "I want to make sure I'm giving that person every opportunity to succeed." There's a certain degree of legitimacy to that view, that you do need to provide a reasonable chance for an individual employee to be successful once you hire them. However, as a leader you have a broader responsibility to your team.

By being focused on rehabilitating one particular individual or a small group of individuals, you end up spending the majority of your leadership energy on the people dragging the organization down rather than investing in the people who you should be trying to lift up.

If you were to create a chart of your A, B, and C players (as seen on page 71 in Chapter Three), where would you invest your time? You want to invest most of your time in the A players, who are values aligned and highly productive, because you need to invest in their future growth to keep them A players. You also want to invest in the B players, who are high in values alignment but somewhat low in productivity. For B players, most of your investment should center on training, so a person who shows a lot of promise can learn the skills they need to become A players.

C players should receive less of your time and energy. You want to maximize your energy by focusing on your high-performing and high-potential team members, rather than on the lowest performing ones. I know it sounds insensitive, but it's a necessary component to assessing the needs of an organization and improving upon how it functions. Most organizations spend a larger percentage of their energy dealing with their lowest performers, which demotivates your higher performers. As hard as it may be on a personal level, if someone is not values aligned, that's very unlikely to change and you need to confront the problem head-on before it turns toxic for both the individual and the organization.

SCOUTING THE HORIZON: WHY WORK TRENDS MATTER TO ASSOCIATIONS

For large associations, the struggle to implement cultural changes revolves around the size and complexity of their leadership structure. As a result, their culture—and the ability to assess and manage it—is spread so thin that it almost disappears completely. For most, they are moving too quickly to tune in to the organization's identity (i.e., its Core Purpose and Core Values) or are not in tune with each other. Then again, in a disjointed structure that pushes rising workloads onto policy-bound workers, people may not want to tune in; they may want to tune out. That's a problem. For any organization to be successful, it needs its people to be successful first. They need to feel good about the job they are doing or they will just stop showing up, in whatever way that may be.

Keeping an ear to the changes occurring in the modern workplace is one of the best ways to improve any amount of sluggish or disjointed systems within their own organizations. When we do turn to the for-profit sector, the future workplace is looking radically different from most of today's work cultures and management structures.

Workers, for instance, are often virtual with one another, living in different cities, different countries, sometimes without ever seeing one another at all. Then there are the multimillion-dollar companies built in a matter of years that have revolutionized the corporate image, replacing office buildings and cubicles with bright, open spaces and trading in the pant suit or tie for a T-shirt and some sweatpants.

Younger companies crave innovation, and, because creativity can be stifled in cramped, bland spaces, you see many of them opting for any office space but an office. But it's not just aesthetics that are changing the workplace. Bold, nearly shocking management choices are sounding alarms for organizations trying to determine where the trends are leading them. And, just as importantly, whether their young workers and recruits are chasing after them.

What's clear is that most workplaces are getting smaller. Young organizations often come in the form of start-ups born in a garage or basement on crowd-sourced capital, and upgrading to little more than a warehouse or trendy downtown apartment. Internal structures are changing just as much. Whether it pertains to marketing, like the **conscious capitalism** model that has become a popular concept to today's consumer, organizations are more or less reinventing the work structure entirely. Take, for instance, Zappos' **holocracy** model, GitHub's **flat organization** structure, or Gravity Payments

CEO Dan Price's **employee wage equality** experiment. The work is moving faster, central workplaces are decreasing, and traditional management strategies are updating themselves to keep up with the changes.

Most organizations leading these types of workplace changes are doing so by thinking more broadly about the role their business plays, or can play, in the world around it. The concept of **inclusion** has become incredibly important, as leaders recognize the benefits of expanding their market reach, while shrinking the borders within their internal structures to assist in workers growing to become more dynamic players with the most diverse set of thoughts.

At its core, leadership should be about growing people through business, rather than growing business through people. This is a nod to the idea that a worker bringing their whole selves to the job actually makes them more valuable to both the organization and themselves. When it's conveyed consistently and sincerely that workers are capable individuals, they often feel a greater sense of importance and responsibility to the organization. Additionally, when each person's contributions are regularly recognized and supported, the workforce is elevated to a communal mind-set, and the expectation of a boss that must decide everything all the time is de-emphasized.

At its core, leadership should be about growing people through business, rather than growing business through people.

That de-emphasis also helps to minimize any feeling among the workforce that their leader(s) is high atop a figurative mountain peak from which they'll never be seen, much less reach themselves.

Instead, a more connected and nurturing kind of leadership can take root, one that's capable of raising everyone up together.

That doesn't mean there are free lunches, though. When given more inclusion in the decision process, workers are also given an increased sense of responsibility and accountability in the work that follows. This brand of leadership isn't necessarily breaking new ground, but giving people the opportunity to be successful on their own. This also means they have to be allowed to fail—so long as they learn from it. That shift in control needs to be explained to leaders thoroughly, taking the time to educate the executive leadership and managers on what they can expect both in terms of successes and failures related to a flatter, transparent hierarchical structure.

Relinquishing some of management's grip on daily tasks also means that deadlines, milestones, and goals have to be made clear from the beginning. Because you're ceding some control, leaders will need to have trial runs as their managerial involvement evolves. Team members' independence should be measured before dictating a task such as, "Okay, complete this project by the first of July; see you when it's done." If a worker is not used to being an independent worker, or they weren't clear on how to accomplish the task given to them, they will almost certainly fail to meet the deadline and the expectation. Leaders need to monitor how their workers are dealing with the freedom to work independently, giving more structure to those that require it.

If you give them more ownership of the work and its outcomes, then they will actually do a much better job. But there's certainly tensions to expect in getting there, as well as in understanding how different people work and the level of individual oversight they may need. Good leaders know that. They have already learned that they can leave some workers to their own devices, and, more often than not, they already know who those workers are. But members of the executive team still need to assist in helping to create a space in which workers and managers can enact a more customizable management strategy.

As people change, the organization itself changes. If its structures are too rigid, the organization cannot evolve accordingly and it will eventually find that it's unable to sustain itself because it cannot cultivate growth. By replacing very fixed structures with a flexible framework that can better accommodate your company's progress, organizations can avoid restricting or limiting their own improvement. Ultimately, Core Values lead the way and frame what is considered required and acceptable behavior, and what is not. Flexibility is derived from this simple model. New ideas like "unlimited paid time off" can be adopted only once you have a clear set of values that are being lived on a daily basis. Accountability breeds flexibility, since it allows you to manage to the results rather than the inputs. Instead of measuring time spent, you measure the outcomes being achieved. Efforts are clearly important and are known by the team, but accountability is for when a great outcome is achieved in alignment with the organization's values.

As business models are changing, some portions of your staffing model will need to change, too. For instance, you can utilize freelancers and independent contractors to explore a new market, or to test a new aspect of the market you're currently in. You can do that in a low-risk way with people who you think have the skills the company may need, without having to hire or fire anyone.

In general, for-profit companies are moving toward a kind of temporary change, wherein freelancers might work on a temporary basis to help the company explore different options without either one having to commit to a salaried position. In that sense, the outer edges of the organization (i.e., target audience, recruitment pool, products and services, partnerships, etc.) are dotted rather than walled. Just as well, their internal structures are becoming more accordion-like, with the organization swelling and contracting, depending on their projects and needs.

Throughout all of these assessments—measuring changes to staff, culture, consumer base, and your organization's relation to the larger business ecosystem around it—maintaining the consistency and transparency of communication surrounding values alignment, goals, and the purpose of the company should be a top priority for leaders. The collaborative culture you're hoping for won't be as powerful if the environment that houses it can't support it. Discord will eventually manifest itself in one way or another within the workplace instead. A work environment that encourages creativity and honesty gets conversations started. The one that supports the collaboration needed to build on those conversations gains the most from them, and ultimately the results it's looking for, too. This environment naturally and necessarily extends to volunteer leadership, board members, committee participants, and the membership at large over time. It's critical that the culture that is being built is consistent within and outside of the organization's paid staff.

CHAPTER WORKSHOP

» As people change, the organization itself changes. If structures are too rigid, the organization cannot evolve accordingly and it will eventually be unable to sustain itself. Obtain feedback from staff and members (e.g., surveys, guided face-to-face group sessions, anonymous digital platforms) to better gauge where the organization's stress points are and dedicate resources to repairing them before their problems worsen.

» Leadership should work to replace very fixed structures with a flexible framework that can better accommodate the progress the organization requires. A fluid work structure allows management at all levels to engage the workforce in more effective ways, affording customizable solutions to individual challenges. Thus, fluidity supports productivity.

» Combining generational, economic, legislative, and technological events, the freelancer movement has become a popular work alternative. For stable and low-risk to companies looking to navigate a changing landscape, freelancer pools are an increasingly valuable talent option to utilize—particularly when considering experiments in areas where you lack the in-house skill or bandwidth.

Chapter Five

BENEFITS OF A HEALTHY ORGANIZATIONAL CULTURE

Teamwork is the ability to work together toward a common vision. The ability to direct individual accomplishments toward organizational objectives. It's the fuel that allows common people to attain uncommon results.

—ANDREW CARNEGIE

If you saw it from afar, Sunny Knoll EcoFarm probably wouldn't look any different from the surrounding northern Virginia landscape: swaying pastures of green and gold, specks of red barns and warped rows of weathered fence, wavy foothills thick with fog and forest sprouting from the backdrop. All the kind of idyllic rural beauty one can imagine is there, enough so that the fifteen-acre farm becomes surprisingly ordinary and slips past the casual passerby into obscurity.[14] But there's something even more idyllic happening at Sunny Knoll, something so remarkably different that you would have to see it up close and for a great length of time to really understand how it works.

At Sunny Knoll, the animals themselves carry out nearly every aspect of day-to-day operations, with a little help from nature and good timing. Overseeing the operation is a young couple, one a Princeton PhD in ecology and evolutionary biology and the other a quality control expert. Together, they act as a conductor leading its figurative orchestra into the right direction at the right tempo. The concept they use to run Sunny Knoll is known as permaculture to some, self-sustaining agriculture to others, both of which roughly translate to the notion that choreographing the natural tendencies of plants and animals is healthier and more efficient than attempting to control them by artificial means.[15]

For instance, when the couple noticed their cows were suffering from diseases and infections caused by parasitic insects, they introduced chickens—a natural insect predator—to the grazing grounds.

Their plan worked, but something else happened, too. The constant pacing from the chickens began spreading the manure around the pasture, thus aiding both its decomposition and acting as a more evenly balanced fertilization for the grass.

When they introduced pigs, the pair realized that the animals' rooting through soil in search of food could replace the need for tilling prior to planting seeds. And when snails and slugs posed a threat to their crops, ducks were brought in for their expertise in hunting them down. Conducting it all requires little more than

---

14   "About," Sunny Knoll EcoFarm, accessed April 30, 2018, http://www.sunnyknol-lecofarm.com/the-ecofarm/.

15   Ibid.; "The Farmers," Sunny Knoll EcoFarm, accessed April 30, 2018, http://www.sunnyknollecofarm.com/the-farmers/.

routinely rotating pastures to help facilitate regrowth and protect the health of the animals, thus ensuring the productivity of the farm itself.

In biology, it's akin to **mutualism**, that coexistence of differences to support the survival of all, a phenomenon that takes place so often you'll see it all around you. Plants, animals, humans, and microscopic matter of all varieties use their natural abilities for the mutual benefit of one another, effectively safeguarding the immediate survival of each other and their offspring. You see it in the oxpecker perched atop cattle, feeding on ticks and other parasitic insects the larger animals can't reach. And when a predator springs into attack, it's the oxpecker, with its keen awareness, its swiveling head and elevated position, that leaps first and screams out to alert its companion. You see it between dolphins and fishermen too, both working in unison—one from below, the other from above—corralling large schools of fish capable of feeding their respective communities. And in a time mostly foreign to many of us now, you see mutualism between humans and dogs. Both have worked together for centuries in a hunt for a shared prey or protection from a common predator.

For many scholars, it's this symbiotic relationship between humans and nature that best explains our survival amid the extinction of our pseudo-related counterparts. It was our ability to adapt to change, organize, collaborate with our surroundings, learn, and create that drove our advancements and continues to lead our progress to this day. Without using the tools, resources, and abilities from one another and our surroundings quickly and aptly, we would perish in harsh environments rather quickly.

Apply that same mind-set to organizational culture and you have the basis for culture's importance as a whole. Managing an organization as something of a living organism is still relatively new ground, but business as a whole is moving away from the impersonal and homogenous, in favor of the personalized and experiential. Why? Well, perhaps the primary reason is the changing of common job types and functions.

As organizations have begun experimenting more and more with emerging and sometimes complex business strategies (e.g., conscious capitalism, holocracy, social media marketing, tech-based products/services, international operations, generational engagement, etc.), they have also become more dependent on the types of "knowledge individual" (i.e., people with an above-average knowledge of how to handle and use information, often independently) that these strategies require. But as author and management thought leader Dan Pink first noted in his 2009 book, *Drive: The Surprising Truth about What Motivates Us*, motivation in most complex fields must come from a mix of autonomy, mastery, and purpose.

We'll talk more about Dan's work later, but what's important here is to understand that the best and brightest of a field are likely to be motivated by intrinsic factors more so than extrinsic ones. As a result, organizations are finding it increasingly difficult to operate, much less scale, purely based on the traditional model of navigating by extensive rules and policies that are often codified in such a way that make them very difficult to change. It would seem people want their brains back, seeking freedom to express their creativity by operating in a transparent and free manner with accountability for outcomes rather than the minutia. More organizations today know they should oblige if they want to capitalize on the opportunities of the times. But to do so, leaders need to tap into a kind of "organizational DNA," or culture, to guide all decision-making and define the rights and wrongs specific to the business, while staying more or less out of the way.

Culture should not narrow your view, nor should its creation or display be insular. It should have an effect on, and be inspired by, the real world. The organization's cultural center should be its staff and its members in equal measure. In other words, association cultures should be inspired by and modeled after the people and things that we strive to be or achieve ourselves: smart, funny, creative, expressive, helpful, beautiful, hopeful, and ambitious, among others.

A good culture is not rigid or polarizing. It should clarify your organization's view and purpose and expand its capabilities. It tells the story, your story, by providing context and nuance to the organization's identity. That story is how everyone attached relates their own culture and purpose in the world to the organization. Culture must be understood to encompass your internal behaviors along with the way you operate and are seen in the public. Members, and even people outside of your membership demographic, need to align with the cultural ideology you put in place, or you will have a mismatch in setting priorities and finding a good operational rhythm.

Key Traits of a Great Culture:

- Inspired by the world outside the organization.

- Mutually beneficial to both the organization and those that it interacts with and serves.

- Everyone connected to the organization knows its Core Purpose.

- Internal staff and your external audience (i.e., current members and the public as a whole) understand the organization's set of Core Values.

In organizational management, a mutually beneficial system that sustains itself with relatively low maintenance is the ideal. When an organization recognizes itself as a sum of many moving, but grating parts, mutualism in the workplace must follow before the workforce grinds itself to halt. Without a real effort to understand, integrate, and support your people (i.e., staff, volunteers, members, and the communities connected to the association's work), their many parts quickly begin to work separately, often in opposite directions, with most never having their full potential recognized, much less their most beneficial assets utilized.

For most leaders, myself included, the act of getting in touch with so many people individually first appears as a kind of complicated machine with a seemingly endless panel of buttons, dials, switches, and levers. A foreign list of codes and instructions further impedes learning how the vast range of functions and capabilities can be used in their totality, almost dooming the operator to a usage that's tedious at best and financially harmful at worst. For today's information worker, for instance, dials and switches are replaced with following rote policies and procedures that can't possibly take into account all of the subtleties of actual operations that the employee needs to navigate. Extensive policies and procedures aim to standardize and reduce risk, and ultimately stifle thinking and innovation.

That isn't to say that all policies and procedures are bad. Rather, some that provide guidance and, of course, have regulatory compliance roles, are critical. However, with a strong culture rooted in purpose and aligned through values, you can dispense with many of the micro-managing details often found in policies and rely on the day-to-day ingenuity that resides in your team's collective mind, but often remains locked up.

Most organizations today use the functions they're most familiar with, or perhaps have the easiest access to, rather than risk pressing the wrong buttons. A lack of willingness to trust staff, take small risks in trying new ways to reach members, and ensure that their people have access to great training and support, often results in poor decision-making and limited professional growth.

By effect, people are often grouped into a glob mentality with no individuality or humanism attached to them at all. However, a meaningful Core Purpose and a well-lived set of Core Values act as a manual informing the operator on how to discover and nurture the hidden advantages of the people in and around the organization, unlocking the broader contributions they've yet to utilize. In other words, values act as road signs, helping everyone on the team make the best decisions at each turn. This sounds extraordinarily vague compared to the safety that a super-detailed set of policies and procedures might provide. Yet, over time, values can be incredibly clear and do become the operating system for the organization.

Realizing that the organization as an entity does not live in a vacuum is critical to understanding how it really exists. Every organization is part of an ecosystem that is much bigger than itself, creating ebbs and flows that can send it sailing out to new places, or sink it where it lies.

Associations are also interconnected, both internally and externally, now more than ever. Learning how to use and engage the particular ecosystem around you can benefit and inform your association's policies, culture, retention, development, member relations, innovation, production, and most importantly, the overall well-being of the association and the people it serves.

This is, after all, about people in the end. The more apt an association is at giving meaning to its workplace, purpose, culture, and policies, the more creative, informed, empowered, and satisfied its people will be. I'm sure I don't need to reiterate the benefits of a happy, purposeful, and empowered worker, but can you imagine what a whole community of them could accomplish? What would that environment look and sound like? What would be made there? What's holding you back from getting there?

> *I'm sure I don't need to reiterate the benefits of a happy, purposeful, and empowered worker, but can you imagine what a whole community of them could accomplish? What would that environment look and sound like? What would be made there? What's holding you back from getting there?*

It's a matter of taking small steps to reach where you want to go, no matter how far it may be. And, as you do, always lead with your tenets first.

As far as the internal workforce is concerned, employees, contractors, and volunteers are still likely to come and go, as shifting and restructuring at both the organizational level and the individual level continue in large measure for the foreseeable future. Associations can benefit from utilizing contractors as their ranks heave with the changes, using them when they need them. Or they can work more aggressively to develop their internal talent by diversifying their training and moving them from a single-function job to a high-potential career track as a way of strengthening their individual value. That choice depends on the limits of an organization and the efforts it's willing to make for the person in question.

In that way, organizations must learn to focus on individuals—working harder and longer to optimize the organizational culture, environment, and development system to get the most from each and every person within it.

As I said before, organizations will require a more flexible framework to allow for better collaboration and support, while staff and leaders alike will be taking on a more diverse set of functions. Likewise, team members will also have to take on more responsibility and initiative. Ensuring that the leadership is able to engage them early, support their training, and track their progress as they work to develop themselves will be critical.

LEARN TOGETHER, GROW TOGETHER

When it comes to collectivizing progress, there's an expression attributed to Harry S. Truman that really hits the nail on the head for me: "Not all readers are leaders, but all leaders must be readers." I read between one and two business books a month. I know many people who read more than that. We do that because we know that if we're not trying to learn something new, we are failing the organizations we lead. We also do it because we are curious, and we want to find out what else is out there, wanting to look around the next corner of the journey and see what may lie ahead. I also know that if I don't bring the rest of my team on the learning journey with me, I am failing them as well as myself.

Leaders, and people in general, who don't want to learn have a fixed mind-set (fixed mind-sets are terrible for growth) and cripple not only the leader's power to invoke progress, but also the entire organization's opportunities for finding a better way. It doesn't mean growth can't occur; a single-engine can still propel a plane forward. But it will be harder to control as the organization expands. When organizations grow, their focus often broadens. Your consumer base, client/member profile, staff, policies, and the markets that impact them, all widen and change as a result of outstanding growth. Eventually, though, that single-engine mentality will only propel the organization into a tailspin.

The number one predictor of an impending tailspin of this type is if the leaders project an unbridled ego. A healthy ego is important for leaders at every level, of course. They need confidence to lead others and execute difficult tasks. It's when egos get out of check, and cultures celebrate a "hero worship" type of view of leaders, that the fixed mind-set sets in. Few people readily acknowledge they have a fixed mind-set, but many leaders who have been successful, particularly when they've had few failures in their history, increasingly believe they have the answers and fail to listen and learn. Bringing humility back to the corner office, and to every level of an organization, is one of the most critical needs for today's associations and commercial entities.

People who make it to the top of an organization—whether as the CEO, the owner of a business, or the executive director of an association—often rely too much on themselves. They view themselves as the boss, and believe that whatever they think and say should be written in stone, even when the weight of such a mentality becomes too heavy and the mistakes begin to pile up. A fixed mind-set inherently becomes narrower with growth, rendering one's once great ability to solve problems and fuel growth incredibly limited. As it's been said many times, two heads are better than one. Why not take advantage of that fact? You have more to gain than you have to lose.

It comes down to cohesion, a pivotal component of all great cultures. You might say that a team that learns together, stays together. When leaders foster an environment of learning, they enable their team to take an active part in the organization's development. By allowing everyone to contribute new ideas, strategies, and tools, you're providing more chances for a problem to get solved. Perhaps even more importantly, by listening and leading with questions instead of answers, leaders can spot new opportunities more readily.

Leaders need to be examples of growth by constantly learning and sharing with their team what they have learned. And while it may not be possible to give a fair testing period to everyone's ideas, a leader who is receptive to the input of others creates an atmosphere that encourages people to contribute as much as they can to their work.

> *Perhaps even more importantly, by listening and leading with questions instead of answers, leaders can spot new opportunities more readily.*

At Aptify, after some years of growth, I found that I fell victim to my own success and wasn't doing a good job at listening. It took a meeting with one of my long-time team members in which they called me out, and shared with me that they felt our meetings were often one-directional—in that I was more interested in lecturing the team than listening to them. While the team did gain value from my insights, I was stifling input from others. I reflected on this and came up with two methods that I used personally and asked my team to implement:

- **Listen and ask questions before sharing your opinion.** Often times a person taking the risk to present a new and contrary viewpoint or idea is shut down because one or more people in the room quickly shoots holes in it. That results in the best idea losing out to the idea(s) of the most stubborn person in the room. The key here is truly listening before asking any clarifying questions. Don't spend time thinking about what you're going to say in response to someone when they speak. Instead, use the time to hear what they have to say and formulate your questions. After you've had this exchange of questions and answers, it's fine to share your views, but this extra oxygen being thrown into the process allows a fledgling idea to have at least a chance of taking hold in a discussion.

- **Debate**. The goal behind this tactic is to get everyone in the room to listen and consider the new idea fully. After the Q&A is complete, each person in the room is required to argue both for and against the new idea. By requiring everyone to debate both sides of the topic, they have to expend intellectual and emotional capacity to really think through the ideas. It's amazing how often you'll find people switching their views as you go through this exercise.

I'm not suggesting you use these two methods in every meeting you have in which a new idea surfaces. For instance, if a staff member suggests changing the location of the coffee pot in the kitchen, you certainly wouldn't want to spend this kind of time on it. But imagine if a team member came in and said, "Hey, I think we should allow non-members to write articles for our journal." If your organization had a long-held belief that only members could be published in your journal, this might seem sacrilegious. Using one or both of the methods noted above would help—the more controversial an idea, the more important it is to apply these methods so you don't squash innovative possibilities before they have a chance to get started.

Whether it's a book, a talk, or even a crisis or accomplishment, everyone takes away something different from every experience. Share what you learned and encourage others to do the same. You never know where a great idea may come from, and it may come at just the time you need it.

One of the best ways comes from the mind of a friend of mine, Arnie Malham, who introduced me to the idea of establishing a company book club in a novel way. Arnie ran an advertising firm for law firms, a field in which creativity and collaboration are critical tenets of a business's success. To help support these values, he built a culture at his firm around two main questions: "How do you grow your team?" and "How do you help the team learn as much as possible?"

Whether it's a book, a talk, or even a crisis or accomplishment, everyone takes away something different from every experience. Share what you learned and encourage others to do the same.

A devoted reader, Arnie thought that a book club sounded like a great answer for both of these questions. The problem, however, was finding a way to get the rest of his team to go happily along with an idea that would require more of their time and energy outside of the office. Arnie's solution? Pay them to read.

It wasn't a lot of money, mind you. An individual could earn somewhere between $200-300 a year by reading. But his theory was that if he gave them a little money to read, he would incentivize them to learn. By reading more, he thought, they would be smarter, better employees. They would grow as individuals and be more fulfilled in their jobs. That, in turn, would make them an even stronger contributory force to the firm's creative demands.

Arnie implemented his plan, setting up a library of sorts in his office. Rather than having a "Book of the Month" format like most book clubs, Arnie told his team they could choose any book they wanted from the library. Each book had approximately three different categories based on the length of the book, with each assigned a specific point value. Arnie also built a database to keep track of who was reading which title. When a person completed a book, they filled out a brief summary of the title and reported what they got out of it. Based on the number of points an individual accumulated over a month or a quarter, they received a certain amount of money.

With the help of his database, Arnie could determine which of his team members had read the same books. If ten people read *Good to Great* by Jim Collins and another five people read *Drive* by Dan Pink, for example, Arnie could pair them into their respective groups for a discussion around what they learned from these books and how they could apply that knowledge to whatever project they happened to be working on at the time.

Arnie ran that book club for more than ten years, while his organization and the teams within it grew stronger, closer, more efficient, and more productive because of it. It all started because of Arnie's passion for reading and learning new things, but it was his leadership intuition that told him he needed to share that gift with all of the team members. Arnie recently wrote a book of his own called *Worth Doing Wrong* that chronicles his journey in growing his business and describes his Book Club concept in much more detail.

Since you're reading this book, I know you understand the benefits of reading. But maybe you're not as familiar with the inner workings of a book club and the benefits that come from them. A book club can be set up in a lot of different ways, but their goal is always the same: read, share, listen, and learn.

To start your own, you can do what most people do and have team members rotate in selecting a title for everyone to read every month or every quarter. At the end of the allotted reading period, get everyone together to discuss the book. This can be done in person, by phone, or video chat, but it's best to make sure the discussion takes place in a verbal format. Most people will not want to write a full summary of their thoughts, much less take the time to read everyone else's notes. It's much easier and more productive if everyone can join in a live discussion to exchange their thoughts. The problem with this approach is it limits choice and you'll likely find that book clubs of this style have very limited participation.

In my view, the better alternative is to take a page from Arnie's playbook and implement a book club that empowers your team to self-select interesting titles at the frequency of their choice. Arnie recently launched a new business, called BetterBookClub.com, which provides you the tools to implement this style of book club in your business, association, or even with social groups. BetterBook-Club.com does a great job of helping you keep track of your team, what they're reading, have read, and share accumulated knowledge and insights from the process. Rewarding your team for reading is an optional component, but it's a fun and inexpensive way to "gamify" the experience and provide a small financial reward to incentivize people. Ultimately, if you want to build a culture that is serious about learning on a continuous basis, a book club of this style is a fantastic facilitator of growth while keeping your team aligned in the process.

LEADING FROM THE BOW

At the root of every successful cultural decision is great leadership. By that, I don't mean that you should subscribe to the traditional "trickle down" attitude. Rather than the belief that all change must come from the top-down, genuine cultural changes actually grow in all directions. Whatever strategy an organization chooses to take to improve its culture, its leaders must take an active and visible part in it.

> *Rather than the belief that all change must come from the top-down, genuine cultural changes actually grow in all directions. Whatever strategy an organization chooses to take to improve its culture, its leaders must take an active and visible part in it.*

Imagine how well Arnie's book club would have done had he said to his team, "I don't ever read business books because I'm above that. I'm the CEO of the company, after all. I've done really well for myself in business, so obviously I don't need to do this, but you guys do." I'm betting the reception would have fallen flat. When the leader is actually doing the stuff they're promoting and showing his or her team that they're always learning and listening, it changes the game. People want someone they know will be receptive to their needs and concerns, not dismiss them or punish them for speaking up. They want a leader who is confident and driven, not cocky and lazy. They want a leader they can learn from, someone who believes in them and inspires them to push themselves further than they would on their own. Most of all, what people want is a leader capable of delivering them and the rest of their team to victory.

When people believe in their leaders and have the right guidance from them, they rally around them and work beyond the call of duty to push the organization forward in whatever way they can. That's the mark of a strong culture, one that allows the leadership to focus on the horizon knowing that they have a team behind them that's willing and able to take them wherever they want to go.

How a leader prepares themselves for growth will determine whether they succeed or fail at garnering the respect and confidence of a team or organization in transition. When you're learning constantly, one thing you figure out rather quickly is that, in spite of whatever success you have had, you're only at the beginning of the journey. What may surprise you, however, is that this is a good thing. You read that correctly. A beginner's mind-set is actually a very powerful tool when it comes to improving culture.

Rather than assuming that you're the expert on a particular issue or problem, if you assume that you're a beginner, it opens up the possibility of learning more. The more you think about something, the harder it is to learn more about that topic. That may lead you to merely pretend—and you may even convince yourself that it's true—that you know everything about the topic in question because you believe that you, as the leader, have to know everything about everything. Not only is this not true, other people know it, too. They can see right through the pretense, and the know-it-all façade only makes them lose confidence in your leadership as well as respect for you as a person and a leader.

At Aptify, one of our team members was deeply passionate about finding a way to help our clients get access to more quality apps that could extend the capabilities of the base system. He was active in our professional services group where he saw patterns in which many clients would ask for the same types of abilities. This individual gained the grassroots support of others he worked with to build an "App Store" for the Aptify community. Many of the senior leaders, including me, were skeptical at first. However, we gave this individual enough space to continue his experiment and he proved us all wrong very quickly. Within weeks of its trial launch, a large number of customers had already downloaded apps from the store and were raving about it. We were advancing our Core Purpose, and the icing on the cake was the nice new stream of recurring revenue that this initiative brought into the firm. This individual was able to share his knowledge and learning with everyone else, and it's a great example of innovation and growth coming from all directions if you foster a culture that encourages incremental risk-taking and experimentation.

Adopting a beginner's mind-set makes you as approachable as it does more efficient and trustworthy. It allows you to bring out the expertise that often lies quietly in other people. Under a know-it-all mentality, these same people would assume they are your subordinates and that their knowledge and skills are therefore either insignificant or unnecessary unless called upon. If the leader never calls on them, however, how could anyone ever benefit from their expertise?

When you establish a learning culture, what you're really doing is giving everyone a chance to work at their maximum potential. You're saying that while a person might work in a low level within the organization, they could be really strong in a particular topic and should be able to come forward and teach everyone else something new about it. The key here is generating the most diverse set of ideas.

> *When you establish a learning culture, what you're really doing is giving everyone a chance to work at their maximum potential.*

Diversity of thought doesn't come if you have the same people talking and making decisions all the time. You need to get a wide variety of people thinking, sharing, and have a culture to support this. This extends beyond your staff. Associations have the amazing advantage of being able to mobilize volunteer workforces to support initiatives in committees and task forces. Commercial organizations are rarely able to get that type of engagement. The problem is that committees often end up as echo chambers due to two factors in particular. First, the people selected to committees are often the known and the trusted people—the folks who already have been around sharing their views for some time. The other issue is that committees often operate in a style that terminates innovative ideas. While lip service may be paid to new ideas, there are often one or two "power votes" on the committee who usually represent the status quo and kill many good ideas before they have a chance in this environment. For an association to have a thriving culture of learning, the approach described here has to be extended beyond your physical office to include volunteers, members and even those outside of your membership circle. You don't get that in an environment unless the leader is emanating an open, receptive, and learning-centric tone.

CULTURE BY DESIGN: TALKING ABOUT CULTURE

When people in any type of business throw around words like "culture" and "purpose," it can make some roll their eyes. Culture is a word that many professionals love to ping-pong around conferences and annual meetings without ever picking it up and looking directly at it. They aren't rolling their eyes at real purpose or culture. They are rolling their eyes at all the fluffy stuff that people use as substitutes for real purpose and culture. It's these pre-fabricated culture trends that people are hesitant to talk about, and therefore dismiss as unimportant (such as surface-level management tricks, compromises like beanbag chairs in the waiting room, office dogs, espresso machines, or something else that has become standard fare for the so-called culturally enlightened).

Don't get me wrong. All of those additions can be effective practices to add life to your cultural values, but they are completely meaningless if you're relying on fads and trends to stand in for an authentic culture and the purpose behind the entire organization. Simply put, there are no cultural short cuts or "booster shots." It takes intensive planning, patience, and a genuinely bought-in leadership that's fully competent of and committed to the importance of culture before an organization can reap the benefits of a healthy culture—innovation, teamwork, brand/staff loyalty, and streamlined operations among them. Throwing around heavy, ambiguous words that make board members nod does not cut it. Frankly, it would be better to dismiss the entire approach around values and purpose than to genericize it in this way, as it would be seen simply as checking a box.

Culture doesn't come knocking on the door as a singular epiphany, either. It vines itself slowly throughout your organization, thanks to a lot of effort and care from those within it. It should serve and inspire people to do better work. By offering access to the organization's lifeblood that fuels its work, a healthy culture is the center of gravity for everything your organization does, so long as you know how to talk about culture correctly and motivate your people to carry it out for the long term.

Culture is not the silver bullet for saving, nor growing, an organization. Rather, culture is the vehicle to an organization's transformation, and its continual evolution. Culture is the constant that transcends change in strategy, environment, and everything else.

I will be very clear here in dissuading you from buying into a popular, but misleading belief: culture is not the silver bullet for saving, nor growing, an organization. Rather, culture is the vehicle to an organization's transformation, and its continual evolution. Culture is the constant that transcends change in strategy, environment, and everything else. Designing a culture that spans all layers of an organization demands more than trends and rhetoric. Avoiding a faux culture, which is ultimately useless at best and harmful at worst, requires what I call a "Culture by Design." An intentional, thoughtful culture depends upon a thriving, autonomous, scalable, and competitive environment rooted in purpose and guided by values. It's also only as good as one's ability to recruit supporters and contributors to it.

Every organization has one of two culture types, a **Culture by Design** or a **Culture by Default**. Whether you see your organization's culture, acknowledge it, and work to improve it will determine which type your organization has in place. In most organizations, the culture is there by default, meaning that a culture exists, but at its core, it was not created intentionally. In many other instances, there are embellishments made to a culture for the sake appearing like a Culture by Design, but the core was not designed intentionally and is therefore rather hollow.

Think back to any job interview you have ever had. From the moment you walked through the doors, whether you recognized it or not, your cultural sensors were tingling. Your interaction with the greeter, the décor of the waiting area, the design of the office space, how people were dressed, what kind of drinks might have been offered, how people talked to you and carried themselves. All of these details formed a perception of the organization's culture. They told you how strong the company's brand and purpose were being represented in these public spaces. Everything that you see and hear in an organization is a reflection of the culture of the company, and you're going to take great care in making sure it's a culture you want to be a part of. A Culture by Default is not the kind of place purpose-driven workers, clients, or members want to be.

A true Culture by Design, in contrast, is painstakingly crafted, communicated, and continually reinforced at every layer of an organization. At its core, each pillar of the cultural foundation of the organization is thought through and aligned to provide a stable and powerful base for success.

Culture by Design:

- Core Purpose

- Core Values

- An Envisioned Future

When we find applied innovation, which requires a strong Culture by Design, we see amazing results. We see how the final product changed an aesthetic or even an entire industry. Think of Pixar or Apple, for example. One expanded the visual limits of film, and the other helped to change the role computers play in everyday life by reimagining who could use computers and how. Neither company could have achieved those remarkable accomplishments without an incredible amount of innovation coursing through the organization. Steve Jobs knew that innovation would be vital to these companies reaching their goals and having success in industries dominated by much larger, richer, more established companies. He also understood the power of culture, reasoning that the best way to foster innovation (and thus the success of the company) was to build an organization around culture and not the other way around.

An organization might have a noble mission, but that alone is not enough to overcome people's natural skepticism, particularly of its commercial components. Associations and not-for-profits that are wholly dedicated to missions often have a mission statement that is generic nonsense or, alternatively, it might be unique to the organization, but so wide-sweeping that it's impossible to internalize. Simpler is better when sharing ideological concepts. The actual mission of the association might be deeply meaningful, but when expressed in a convoluted or clichéd way, it becomes that boring plaque on the wall of the boardroom rather than a living part of the organization's culture. Such a misstep occurs when the organization forgets who it is somewhere along the way, and attempts to cover its lack of conviction with a kind of bandage—a generic and unconvincing purpose.

To deliver thoughts around culture and its benefits convincingly, leaders must find ways to simplify the concepts and make them relatable to everyone both inside and outside the organization. To do this, we can use our own lives as a microcosm for how important it is to define our purpose and values. Personally, I try daily to remind myself of my own life's purpose and encourage everyone else to do so as well. Why am I here? What is my purpose in life? Lofty, existential questions like these are common, and they typically lead to a few general answers on which everyone can probably agree, such as, "We're trying to find happiness," or, "We want to live our best life and touch everyone around us in a positive way."

When we tell the stories of influencers and their lives, they revolve around inspiring themes that focus on someone who dedicated themselves to a particular mission of good will. Think of the Kennedy Center Honors when they honor someone's life work. When we present culture as a choice and as something that lives, breathes, grows, and is simultaneously capable of dying, the idea of culture sustaining lasting change sounds counterintuitive to a lot of people. But when we talk about how it forms a legacy (creates a model that others can learn from, contribute to, and be immensely motivated by) culture takes on the image of something capable of transcendence, something that will continue to add value and strength to both the organization and the people connected to it, or its mission, indefinitely.

Most leaders don't want to tumble down the rabbit hole of culture because it's often fundamentally misunderstood and, ironically, underestimated in an industry that claims to thrive on purpose. Establishing a learning program that the leader is actively and visibly a part of is the best way to set the kind of tone that inspires a collegial type of culture in which everyone can find their best assets and help grow the organization. But growth, like so much in organizational management, is only the beginning of a new series of obstacles.

CHAPTER WORKSHOP

» **Culture** is an attitude, a way of living shared values. It's much deeper than the tangible trends and fringe benefits we see so many organizations embracing. The genesis to implementing a particular culture is to first question the purpose of your own life. Then, you must identify the purpose of the organization and how it might align with your life's purpose.

» When people in other professions talk about culture, it's often less scary to people. It seems more natural, typically greeted with a greater curiosity and willingness to talk about culture in fields such as academia and media. Anthropologists, sociologists, journalists, artists, filmmakers, musicians, historians—they all talk about culture, but few get to the root of it. If an organization is not committed to understanding its bigger purpose and building a culture around it, then it will only create a superficial culture that is riddled with contradictions and confusion. Open up lines of communication around the concept of culture and listen to the feedback you receive from both inside and outside the organization to assess where your organization stands on the idea and how it can be improved. There are many ways to strengthen communication and get people to generate new ideas, but the two I've found helpful in this regard follow:

   ▫ **Listen and ask questions before sharing your opinion.** Great ideas and deep personal resolve don't always coexist in the same person. If you want to encourage people to bring their ideas forward, make it a habit to ask at least three clarifying questions that are not biased when a new idea is presented. Some of the questions I've used include, "How would this impact our staff? How would it impact our customers? Does this align with our Core Purpose?" Of course, those are just simple examples.

□ **Debate.** By debate, I don't mean argue. After you have listened to a person or group's idea and exchanged a few clarifying questions and answers, make everyone involved, (regardless of which side of the idea they may be on) argue both for and against the idea. People often take sides too quickly in a meeting when a new idea presents itself. This mental exercise requires people to think about the pros and cons of an idea in a new way, and most often results in a deeper understanding of the idea itself and a change in opinion.

» **The benefits of strong culture.** There are four key benefits to culture that should be communicated clearly and consistently:

1. **Low cost** — Attitude and environmental changes are free or very near to it.

2. **Sustainable** — Culture stimulates new growth while simultaneously helping to nurture the progress an organization has already made by making people (both inside and outside the

organization) want to invest themselves into the organization and its work.

3. **Return on Culture** — A strong, well-articulated culture adds value to the organization in the eyes of its staff, members, and the general public).

4. **Alignment** — Culture is a useful tool in bringing members, potential members, staff, volunteers, and the public together based on such key motivators as: sense of purpose, values, professional needs and interests, and personal convictions.

» **Culture of Learning**

   ▫ A Culture of Learning does four things consistently and pervasively:

      1. Promotes a better understanding of the organization's work and thus greater contributions to its mission.

      2. Embraces change.

      3. Embraces failure when it comes from having experimented in new ways to improve and learn.

      4. Learns one step at a time.

» **Culture by Design**

   ▫ A culture by design has three major parts:

      1. **Core Purpose** — Core Purpose is the true reason why the organization exists. Profit's not Core Purpose. Profit's important, but it's the fuel that drives an organization, not its underlying

reason for being. Core Purpose must be real and meaningful. Every part of what you do as an organization should tie to Core Purpose.

2. **Core Values** — As we covered in Section I, Core Values are the agreed upon *behaviors* that a person or organization will hold themselves up to as they pursue their Core Purpose. Values guide our decision-making, and they should be immutable and non-negotiable.

3. **An Envisioned Future** — Set large goals that you strive toward over a long period of time (ten to thirty years). In their 1994 bestseller *Built to Last: Successful Habits of Visionary Companies*, Jim Collins and Jerry Porras define this type of long-term goal as a "Big Hairy Audacious Goal," or BHAG. The purpose of such a goal is to set a stake in the ground defining where you're going as an organization. It should be something you don't know how to do, but rather are striving to learn about and achieve as a team. Once achieved, BHAGs should be reset using the same criteria.

RASA.IO'S BHAG

By 2030 we will improve the lives of one billion people around the world through better information.

SUGGESTED READING

Worth Doing Wrong by Arnie Melham

Drive: The Surprising Truth about What Motivates Us by Dan Pink

Chapter Six

CULTIVATING SUSTAINABLE GROWTH

Growth is painful. Change is painful. But, nothing is as painful as staying stuck where you do not belong.

—N. R. NARAYANA MURTHY

A number of years ago, the American Alliance of Museums (AAM, formerly the American Association of Museums) decided to take a big gamble on their membership model. The AAM's traditional business strategy was almost entirely membership-funded, and the member was the museum, not the individual museum professional or enthusiast. They operated a sliding scale of membership dues based upon the size of the museum. Large and well-funded members like the Guggenheim, the Met, or the Smithsonian paid very high annual dues to the AAM each year, based on their total annual funding and revenue. Smaller or underfunded museums typically couldn't afford memberships. But, because the AAM's revenue model didn't depend on them anyway, the organization historically didn't focus on their inclusion in events, communications, marketing strategies, and other major initiatives. The smaller groups certainly were welcome, but the business model of AAM wasn't historically designed in a way that allowed them to participate effectively. AAM had been historically successful, but the model was beginning to crack.

Over the years, all that began to change. Their financial position declined as museums around the country experienced funding shortages and fewer visitors, and soon the AAM wondered how it could finance the business any longer. Drastic times called for drastic measures, so the board went outside the box and hired as its new CEO, Ford Bell, a veterinarian by trade who happened to serve on the board of directors for a local museum in his hometown of Minneapolis. Bell was a museum enthusiast, and, along with his unlikely résumé, came a radical new message: the AAM would completely revamp its membership structure to engage everyone and anyone with an interest in advancing museums. They would no longer focus on engaging wealthy museums as their primary method of financing the mission. Their goal was to more effectively embrace the entire population interested in advancing museums. This included all those who were, had been, or who might become members of a museum. Not only did doing so make more financial sense over the long run, it also reconnected the organization to

The AAM would completely revamp its membership structure to engage everyone and anyone with an interest in advancing museums. They would no longer focus on engaging wealthy museums as their primary method of financing the mission.

a deeply meaningful purpose, which had never been emphasized or realized in the past.

"Our new beginning and brand is designed to help us truly unite the museum field—from art museums to zoos and everything in between—so that we may more effectively advocate for the cause of museums," Bell said in a statement upon rolling out the AAM's new direction. "Speaking with one voice, the breadth of the US museum field will be able to make the case that museums are essential to our educational infrastructure, essential to our economic prosperity, and essential to building communities everywhere."

About the decision to change their name from the American Association of Museums to the American Alliance of Museums, chair of the board and COO of the Newark Museum in New Jersey, Meme Omogbai, explained, "By definition, an alliance is an entity forged for the mutual benefit of all. That is the essence of the new American Alliance of Museums—to re-ignite an organization into one whose aim is to benefit all: our museums, the individuals who work in them, and the communities they serve."

Bell elaborated on the name change by drawing a line to organizational purpose. "[O]ur new name signals our resolve to unite the museum field so that we can speak with one strong voice. We are no longer the trade association for museums, but rather the *cause* of museums. Moreover, our new brand goes far beyond mere cosmetics. Our brand as the American Alliance of Museums is emblematic of our commitment to advancing the cause of museums—as well as supporting those who work in museums, donate to them, or simply love them—and the communities served by America's museums."

With their purpose now publicly underscored, AAM announced a new tier of membership for professionals that would be free to join. Any individual in the world working in a museum could join the organization at no cost. The AAM's reasoning behind such a bold decision was to establish itself as the hub of all things related to museums. They wanted to create an open place for everyone to learn more about museums—hoping that by learning more, they would want to become members of, or at least visit, a museum. The AAM was also banking on the idea that their vast collection of information, expertise, news, and museum partners would compel those with an interest in museums and museum-related resources to join their organization. They also knew that the success of all museums was essential to AAM's relevancy, and thus its own success. In other words, the Open Garden Model seemed like the best strategy for their future, having realized the interconnected nature of their business' ecosystem.

Bell and his team also went to the large museum members most responsible for funding the organization in the past and informed them that if they were to take advantage of a free membership right now, the AAM would be gone. They presented their vision for the future of AAM and requested each group maintain their organizational membership. Bell explained that they would receive differentiated benefits over time by helping the AAM with its purpose of advancing the cause of museums in the court of public opinion. He then asked these top members to commit to five years at their current level of funding to achieve their mission—a proposal to which every member agreed. They weren't buying into a great, sure-fire deal exactly; they were buying into a cause they believed in. One they knew that, with enough dedication and vision, would eventually yield better revenue and funding results for the entire museum community.

Over that five-year period, the AAM's individual membership went from basically zero up to somewhere in the fifty thousand range. AAM achieved such an outcome by recruiting more organizational members at the museums it served, offering memberships at much smaller dollar amounts to drive up overall membership as well as member engagement. In the past, if you were the director of a small museum who couldn't afford an AAM membership, you didn't do anything with AAM. But, because AAM opened the door to all, it generated much more revenue from individuals spending comparatively small dollar amounts for courses, certifications, and other benefits. Plus, many new museums joined the organization because of the AAM's decision to offer a lower pricing tier for museum memberships, while the large museums mostly stayed on as members at the higher price level. Bell understood that by opening AAM's doors and rebooting its organizational model, he could expand its presence and gain a much richer set of resources, which ultimately saved the organization from extinction and led it into a new era of prosperity and advancement of its purpose.

Driving the board's decision to hire Bell and go along with this radical vision was financial crisis, perhaps the most powerful motivator of any business. The AAM was also a one-hundred-plus-year-old organization that had run largely in the same way it had since its founding, so it probably never would have changed if it wasn't for the fact that it had to change. The reason the organization managed such a major transition successfully had a lot to do with the leadership team's preliminary work before they actually executed the changes.

Bell, the board, and the executive staff all did their due diligence in assessing the changes that needed to be made, as well as the ways in which they could make them. Much of that research AAM obtained by offering different ways for people to give feedback (as we discussed in Chapter 4), which is crucial to any organization at all times, but especially during periods of significant transition.

Growth is one such period of significant transition. There's a lot that happens when you're trying to inspire people, while simultaneously crafting strategy and goals to drive your business forward. Ultimately, you can't have one without the other—not for long anyway. An inspired but directionless organization will eventually dissolve itself just as surely as a methodical but uninspired one will. It's an art to manage the balance that draws upon facilitation/influence skills, instructional design, and change management to both advance the organization's growth and maintain the ground it has already gained. At its best, a vibrant Culture by Design will feed your strategy and vice-versa.

Many associations have historically been so fixated on maximizing the professional success of their members that they stop the wheels of innovation and progress once they feel they have fulfilled their role as a professional networking and development resource. They mostly don't challenge themselves to go beyond that role and see what else the strength of their network could provide people both inside their association and the larger community around it. But as a healthy culture begins to attract new and different people, associations must be prepared to handle a shifting landscape both internally and externally.

Steering an organization through momentous change positions leaders in the thick of a cultural revolution, as well as on the edge of an administrative minefield. At times, you may even feel like you've landed on a strange new planet, where decisions will either revive and invigorate the organization or lead it into chaos, mutiny, or worse. It's at that crossroads where leadership makes all the difference.

Good leaders know how to influence successful outcomes. Chances are, you haven't achieved positive results in your career without understanding the dynamics of people. Maybe it's intuitive, maybe it's learned, but leaders at any level know how to inspire others to follow and support them once they do. They know that stable growth depends upon their ability as a leader to match company goals and directives to the organization's culture. Good leaders know how to both inspire change and guide people through it once they do.

THE MIND-SET OF CHANGE

Change is never easy for anyone. I don't want you to think that redesigning commonly held business and personal beliefs has been easy for me, nor should you think that doing such a thing will be easy for you. But if you don't like change, you're going to like irrelevance even less.

Change will always be harder for those most familiar with what's being replaced—at least until they see just how much better things can be once the changes occur. Unfortunately, the kind of corporate structures of the past slowly installed a homogenous environment that we're still working to untangle, trying in earnest to identify exactly what works and what doesn't in both organizational management and a rapidly evolving modern society.

Perhaps the most costly loss to associations in such a model is the chance for staff and members alike to feel like they're important enough to the organization to invest more of themselves. Then again, the chance to be part of an innovative and meaningful environment—where they're more likely to discover ways to do their job better and contribute to both their own and the organization's impassioned purpose—is a significant loss as well.

Refusing to jump when there's no certainty of where you'll land is a natural instinct for anyone. Because of that fact, many people will hold on to structures or practices they know are becoming obsolete and habits they know they should break. Associations, in particular, have a tendency to avoid change because they're afraid of the risks incurred by going against traditions, norms, and sometimes antiquated bylaws. No matter what kind of organization you may have in mind, habitual thinking and the disparities of attitudinal differences play the biggest roles in one's ability to alter habits and break from traditions while still adhering to Core Values and manifesting a unified purpose. But for many associations, it's now more of risk for them not to change than if they do.

There are a seemingly infinite number of elements involved when it comes to implementing new policies or attempting to change old mind-sets. Renovating a work environment is a massive, yet gradual transformation, so take it slowly. Understand that mind-set is the thinking culture of your organization. It's the mental expression of the purpose your organization rests upon, and the values it's guided by. Perhaps more importantly, mind-set generates the behaviors that become the organization's culture. The values an organization possesses go into the policies it composes, which are ultimately dictated by the mind-set of the leadership and the culture it wishes to create. Everything needs to be supported and expressed purposefully, as people want to see verifiable proof that the culture and mind-set of the organization is alive and well. Culture is like any living organism in that you must keep it nourished to sustain and grow over time. Just as well, culture is a habit that requires repetition and finding new ways to keep your values and purpose alive is a critical role for leaders.

The flexibility of the association's internal and external structures is another important feature to include in your organizational mind-set. By that I am referring to the expression of cultural elements, depending on whatever type of culture you have, through policy. The flexibility an organization can show outwardly helps convey respect and trust for the individual, even engendering a greater sense of responsibility and pride for the work they do.

When policies can accommodate personal preferences and needs openly, it's a gesture of recognition and concern for the people beholden to them that not only boosts individual performance, but also collective morale. The mind-set you set should be inclusive and adaptable to the organization's environment and marketplace, but it should also treat people on an individual level in the very same manner. The outcome ultimately creates the most long-term benefit in the form of diversity of thought. In that way, structural flexibility is focused on understanding and accommodating people's preferences in order to better engage them as the organization grows and adapts to external changes. However, organizations that implement structural flexibility superficially can sometimes find themselves with bigger problems than existed when they offered no flexibility at all.

For instance, if internal policy says a team member can do something but leadership doesn't work to enforce it or protect the individual from penalties, then the individual obviously doesn't actually receive the flexibility benefits and is likely to feel misled, or even abused. For workplace flexibility to be effective, it has to be implemented thoroughly, genuinely, and followed up on consistently. Otherwise, you will not get the mutual benefit of engaging team members completely by helping them to feel respected, valued, and trusted. It's going to be an exercise in frustration on both sides, so the benefits and costs must be understood and explained at all levels.

THE STRUCTURE OF YOUR ENVIRONMENT: SHOULD IT STAY OR SHOULD IT GO

Enriching the work environment is a very multi-faceted process tying culture, structural flexibility, personalization, incentives, and so many more elements together in hopes of creating a healthier habitat in which an organization can grow stronger.

You should also keep in mind that there are many things about traditional structures that people don't want to change, and some, especially in associations, simply can't be changed even if they did. No business wants to go backward. Surely no leader wants to intentionally shrink their organization and send team members to the unemployment line or fall short of their members' expectations.

Likewise, there are many good things that a well-managed, traditional structure can offer. It can afford workers with great pay and benefits, solid job stability, provide clear directives to follow, and offer fluid channels to ascend through if well-defined goals are reached. Likewise, a traditional structure can offer members some degree of built-in knowledge around the kinds of benefits, resources, fee system, and general operations they are likely to encounter. But knowing which elements of old to keep and which elements of new to adopt requires an abundance of research and trial-and-error before an organization gets the lush work environment and member engagement it may be hoping for.

So what should you do first? I'm a big fan of an idea that Jeff Bezos of Amazon popularized, which is to visualize the customer and their viewpoint in every decision-making meeting. Early on at Amazon, Bezos was known for having an additional chair in each meeting room that was always empty and represented the customer who wouldn't be there. The team members were required to speak, literally, in the voice of the customer, role-playing and speaking back to the group about how a customer would react to what they were deliberating. The power of this visualization and role-play is that you never stray too far from the customer's thinking and you remember your purpose more clearly, in most cases. It also results in thinking about the customer's needs, wants, and preferences ahead of organizational doctrine and business model inertia.

> The power of this visualization and role-play is that you never stray too far from the customer's thinking and you remember your purpose more clearly.

You can start by identifying what people want and don't want from the association. For example, everyone wants to spend less time on rote/repetitive tasks. Are there things an association can do to save members time? How can we best know where opportunities lie? Perhaps it's best to start by studying the actual lives of some customers to see how best to innovate existing products, or create entirely new ones to help the customer in their journey?

When Toyota was working on the design for its second generation Sequoia, its large family-hauling SUV, it dispatched its head designer to live with an American family for a month. The Japanese man was embedded into the family for a full month. He lived with them, ate with them, drove with them, and learned an incredible amount about how this family used their vehicle, including what worked and what didn't work for them. Beyond that, he learned about aspects of the family's lifestyle that didn't directly affect product design but created an environment for a more empathetic style of listening and observing.

One of the innovations the second generation Sequoia introduced was a class-leading short turn radius. This sounds like a technical feature that wouldn't go far beyond the product details buried somewhere on Toyota's website, but it's an incredibly valuable feature. The large Sequoia (the size of a Chevy Tahoe) can maneuver in and out of tight parking spots, narrow roads, and garages far more nimbly than cars in its class as well as vehicles that are considerably smaller. Toyota likely wouldn't have prioritized this feature if it weren't for the experience of the designer living with the family and seeing how they struggled to maneuver their large vehicle through daily life. This feature wouldn't have been as high on the priority list as things like more cargo room, towing capacity, mileage, etc., had it not been for this customer-centered design approach. Clearly Toyota took this idea to an extreme level, one that their size and resource base allowed, and the outcome was a profoundly better truck. For associations, thinking about the daily lives of members in ways that go beyond what associations have traditionally viewed as their role is one way to think about the opportunities ahead.

Associations can now easily put the idea of customer-centered outreach into action by taking advantage of available technology (such as AI in browsing habits, content aggregation, and the various software and hardware options that make task delegation, global collaboration, and working remotely possible). So many technologies are available to us today that can make our lives more enjoyable and our work more productive. Finding a way to curate the best content for each person in your audience on a daily basis is one of many ways to better engage members and non-members alike.

Your members are probably having a hard time keeping up with news, events, and developments in their field or industry. Your association probably has a newsletter of some sort and attempts to help in this area, but the problem is that each of your members is different with a unique set of needs and interests. Until now you couldn't possibly create a separate newsletter for each person, but with modern AI and related technologies you can easily do this. Aggregating and personalizing industry news and content may not be a traditional area of focus for associations, but it solves a major pain point in the daily lives of the members. Of course, this is but one simple example of how a purpose-driven and customer-centered design process can yield a larger and more engaged audience base. But it's an excellent place to start, given its relatively low-cost, low-risk, high-reward nature.

Internally, organizations can also improve their work environment by adhering to rather simple principles. Managers and leaders that succeed in recognizing and respecting staff at an individual level can amend their policies and build fuller, more interactive relationships that yield greater reciprocity. All organizations run because of people, and the best leaders not only know that, they build their management structure around it.

Depending on how you look at it, designing a flexible work structure is either more or less difficult today than it was, say, twenty or thirty years ago. Positions aren't as permanent or centrally located as they once were, so cultivating a people-centric environment is especially difficult if many of your team members will only remain temporarily or work remotely. If people are not being treated in a familial way, there's a large amount of instability in the environment, which leads to a lack of loyalty and engagement. When the environment is good, people find so much of their loyalty to and engagement through their connection with the organization's purpose, values, and the other people similarly engaged for the same reasons. Hence why so many organizations today are trying to change the overall mind-set of their environment—to give workers and members more to connect to and enjoy.

On the other end, designing a more people-centric environment is easier now than it once was due to a growing number of options that enable us to interact with one another without having to be physically present. Video conferencing, instant messaging, video sharing platforms, virtual forums, broadening internet ranges, improved electronic and physical delivery services—all of these amount to a valuable toolbox for keeping people working together even when apart.

But even with all of the modern conveniences to help us stay connected, none of them do much good if people are not connecting to the same ideas or sharing the same purpose and values. Overcoming that obstacle has to do with bridging different expectations and misunderstandings between workers and the organization, and of course the people that are outside of the walls of the organization are critical to achieving its purpose.

For several years now, workplace flexibility as a concept has been rippling through the corporate sector, though only informally, theoretically, or ineffectually in most cases. For a while, there was also some movement toward adapting policy to different people's work and personal situations, but a lot of that was informal as well and hard to track. As a result, policies became a way to officially enforce these ideas in an effective way and ensure that the workplace was really on board with the different changes. But the kind of top-down, blanket policies that were popular in previous eras didn't work.

A stable, but flexible policy system needs to be thorough in trying to effectively execute upon the organization's collective mind-set and culture. Therefore, policies need to be minified and malleable and people need to be able to adapt within them. Meanwhile, leadership needs to support the simpler and reduced set of policies emphatically and set the example to follow. The goal is to get people to think about how to serve by living the Core Values as their primary set of "policies," policies that direct specific behaviors be limited wherever necessary.

I'll give you an example. In 2014, 429 million vacation days went unused, a statistic that amounts to only about 14 percent of workers using all of their vacation time.[16] Policies were in place to offer workers vacation time, but the purpose behind why these policies existed in the first place had vanished. The US government had spent decades debating whether to create paid-leave laws, but no proposals ever passed. Outside the US, however, paid leave legislation were becoming more common, with some thirty countries adopting them into law by the 1930s. For the US, it was actually the private sector that brought vacations into the workplace in the early 1900s, because their workers were burning out. No one asked, "Should they be allowed to take a vacation?" They were more methodical than that and instead held the view that their workers were assets who need repair. The only way to repair them, as it turned out, was to actually give them paid vacations as matter of a corporate policy.

With the exception of Korea and Japan, the average US worker today works longer hours than workers in any other country. All three countries—the US, Korea, and Japan—have labor markets that average just ten vacation days per year. The labor markets are highly competitive and the standard of living relatively high, resulting in what is essentially a culture of work.[17] The problem is that workers in such a culture become exhausted, unhappy, and ultimately disen-

---

16 "An Assessment of Paid Time Off in the US: Executive Summary," Project: Time Off, last modified 2013, http://www.projecttimeoff.com/research/ assessment-paid-time-us.

17 Alan E., "The Tortured History of Paid Leave in the United States," Pacific Timesheet: TEAL, last modified May 7, 2014, https://blog.pacifictimesheet.com/ blog/how-paid-leave-started-in-the-united-states.

gaged. A number of companies, seeing the mutual benefits of time off, have begun incentivizing vacations in recent years. FullContact, a Denver-based software company, began giving its employees a minimum of three weeks paid vacation time (more is given if needed) and $7,500 cash if they "completely disconnect from work." Full-Contact co-founder and CEO, Bart Lorang, explained the policy to Monster.com, as a matter of supporting organizational culture. "At FullContact, the core value is 'Be Awesome with People.' Since 'worldly' is the W in *awesome*, we encourage people to travel the world," Lorang said. "As a result, I get more productive, happier employees. I would rather have them super-productive and super-charged when they're working rather than constantly at a seventy to sixty percent state."[18]

The CEO of Aetna is another example of beneficial policy-making. After having a terrible ski accident in 2004, Mark Bertolini spent roughly a year out of the office as he fought to recover. In addition to traditional physical therapy exercises, he tried homeopathic techniques, yoga and meditation, as well as some nutritional changes. As a result, he made a much faster and fuller recovery than doctors had anticipated. When he returned to work, he brought in yoga and meditation for everyone. While only 28 percent of people actually took any of the classes, it was so effective in reducing stress and increasing wellness among workers that it decreased Aetna's paid healthcare costs by more than $9 million the following year.[19]

---

18   Caroline Zaayer Kaufman, "6 companies with sweet time off perks," Monster, accessed May 1, 2018, https://www.monster.com/career-advice/article/companies-with-vacation-perks.

19   David Gelles, "At Aetna, a C.E.O.'s Management by Mantra," *The New York Times*, last modified February 27, 2015, https://www.nytimes.com/2015/03/01/business/at-aetna-a-ceos-management-by-mantra.html.

In the US, the private sector is really the driver of many government policies, so it's left up to them to change the way much of the national workplace operates. That's exciting, and it's also why there are some very impactful experiments, and heated discussions, around an organization's approach to policies, how to bring them in, how to get people to take part in them, how to determine if they're achieving good results.

The fact that output as a metric for success, a concept that has shaped much of the private sector's current mind-set and thus environment, is being seriously reconsidered poses some enormous outcomes about which all organizations can only speculate at this point. Nevertheless, we are beginning to see a significant shift in mind-set seemingly everywhere we look as people in nearly every field and industry increasingly ask, "Shouldn't we consider our quality of life and environment, not just volume of output?"

As the mind-set shifts, the policies we can use to meet them will need to be thought through carefully to realize their benefits and ensure they can be enforced. The quality of life and one's work environment should be included in those discussions and tied in to those policies. Inform yourself, be aware of all the changes taking place in the business ecosystem as it relates to your organization. Remember not to disregard a connection too quickly, as you may be surprised to find who and what is linked to your association.

Some of these decisions and findings will impact you more than others, but effective policies depend upon good information and foresight to guide them. To make this work, Core Values need to become ingrained in the daily behavior of your team. A mind-set needs to be embedded that genuinely adapts to changes and policies when needed, and should be reflected within your company to display its possibilities.

CHAPTER WORKSHOP

» **Work to match policies to culture.** A strong organizational structure depends on flexibility as much as it does on clarity. Don't bind yourself and others to excessive or rigid policies, as it limits the organization's ability to pivot quickly when necessary and adapt to external changes. Instead, let your Core Values guide you through the policy-making process.

» **Mind-set is the "thinking culture" of a company.** Mind-set needs to be coherent and aligned throughout the organization. Policies need to be consistent with mind-set and implemented effectively and thoroughly, while recognizing the evolution of governmental legislation, private sector trends, and societal changes/needs.

» **Know your audience.** In order to serve its community most effectively, an association should be in tune with the lives of their members, as well as the people their members interact with. By understanding the connections between the association and its broader community, it's easier to identify what people want and don't want from the association. For example, everyone wants to spend more time doing the things they enjoy. What can the association do to save members time? Everyone wants to advance in their career. How can the association help them do that? Everyone wants to learn more about their passions, and many would like to share that knowledge with others. Can the association find new ways for members to fuel and share their passions with others? Don't limit the context of these questions to the traditional services the association has provided. The questions should be centered around the people alone. Any answer to these questions could be fuel for innovative thinking that might lead to new products, services, partnerships, or other ways of building value for the community.

SUGGESTED READING

Built to Last: Successful Habits of Visionary Companies, Jim Collins and Jerry Porras

SECTION III
THE CROPS

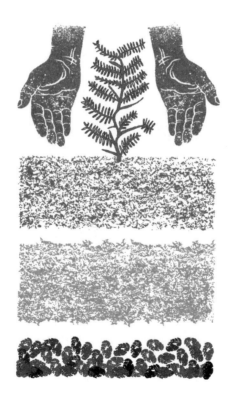

Chapter Seven

FINDING AND ENGAGING YOUR COMMUNITY

Without a sense of caring, there can
be no sense of community.

—ANTHONY J. D'ANGELO

The boundaries of your brand will come to define you. That may sound a little dramatic, but it's the truth. Whether you consciously set those boundaries, or allow them to set themselves without paying too much attention to the thought, is entirely up to you. Regardless of how it gets there, every organization slowly builds a wall around its views on its target market, brand image, and the types of products and services it offers. Everyone has limits, but limit yourself too much and you will eventually doom yourself to stagnated growth or decline. Organizations must be confident and adventurous enough to continuously push the scope of how it views itself, from who it is to who it believes comprises its audience.

Having an understanding of what your product or service is and who it serves is critical to answering difficult questions before tackling new challenges such as, "Does serving this client advance our purpose? What are the risks associated with this client? How much will those risks cost me if they occur? How can I best prepare for this new project so that it's successful and has reusable parts as well? Am I, and my team, able to meet the demands in preparing for those risks?" We have all fallen victim to the temptations of shiny objects in our midst, those projects or strategies illuminated by the allure of more members, bigger revenues, or simply convenience, and we will all probably do it again, too. In those moments, asking ourselves whether we should, or even need to, rarely enters the conversation. But that doesn't mean that thinking more broadly is wrong. In fact, now more than ever, thinking beyond the scope of tradition is essential to an association's future relevancy.

PERSONAL PURPOSE: TOO MANY CHOICES, TOO LITTLE TIME

As we've touched on in earlier chapters, management strategies have begun to tinker with the idea of engaging employee purpose, hoping to connect team members to their jobs in ways that drive productivity and performance toward undeniably positive results. But the trouble with purpose is that it can take a long time for someone to find what theirs is. Some may find it very early in life and pursue it from the start of their education and career, but for most it takes a long time to work it out.

From a management perspective, it's easier to focus on strengths rather than purpose. While purpose is a great thing to look for and something that really drives and excites people, if you can focus on someone's strengths, purpose can be found more quickly. We're moving away from the idea that management should help people mute or attempt to resolve their weaknesses. Many organizations, associations included, are now seeking ways to outsource people's weaknesses if it doesn't come naturally to them and help them improve on their strengths instead. A weakness isn't necessarily something to be ignored or tossed out too quickly, mind you—sometimes weaknesses can be shored up easily with a bit of training and attention. However, focusing on strengths means putting people into positions they'll likely thrive in and enjoy the most. At the same time, this requires being aware of weaknesses rather than covering them up. Potholes in a road aren't as dangerous if they're visible. If they're hard to see due to lighting or weather, they can be extreme hazards. Personal and professional weaknesses are similar. If you seek them out and don't attempt to cover them up, you can work around them and leverage your strengths more effectively.

Most of the time, if you really enjoy doing something, you'll be good at it. Sometimes people are very good at something and they can get paid well for it, but they really enjoy doing something else more. With today's increasingly collaborative and choice-friendly work environment, it's easier for people to do both. Practically speaking, that's beneficial to a person who's either younger and doesn't have that much experience, or someone who's older and never had as many choices in their career.

But the availability of all this choice is not without its drawbacks. Whether people know their purpose or not, many struggle to navigate the wide range of choices now available to them. When it comes to choice and aligning with one's purpose in today's interconnected world, one of the association's primary goals should be to help make people aware of their environment (that is, society and their respective industry in combination) and who they are in relation to it.

> *When it comes to choice and aligning with one's purpose in today's interconnected world, one of the association's primary goals should be to help make people aware of their environment (that is, society and their respective industry in combination) and who they are in relation to it.*

That's a big project. And because most associations don't want to get into deep psychology with their members and staff, they usually find it more efficient to leverage a person's strengths more effectively than to spend too much time and resources trying to support their weaknesses.

THE PRODUCT: TAPPING THE LIFEBLOOD OF YOUR COMPANY

What's more important to you: Knowing the purpose of your product or creating the product of your purpose? It's a bit like the "chicken or the egg" question: you can't create a successful product without knowing what purpose it serves. Not even a painter can create a moving piece of art without knowing what they want to say and having at least a little understanding of how to paint. A product, whether a service or a material good, has to know what its purpose is, which requires understanding who would use it and why. But what if you thought of your product as an extension of your fundamental purpose? By connecting your product to something larger, wouldn't it feel more important, exciting, and authentic than just a thing you're trying to sell?

A parable I've often heard to explain this is a tale of three brick-layers working on a project together. A bystander asked each of the three men a simple question, "What are you doing?" The first man answered, "I am creating a wall." The second man answered, "I am working on a building." The final man answered, "I am building a cathedral that will serve many generations of my community." Which person do you think would be more willing to go the extra mile on that project? Who would take the greatest pride in their work?

In a similar way, the work of the association in delivering its product can be understood to be in alignment with a greater purpose. If you're working on a seminar for your members that is going to help them learn the latest techniques in their field, it likely serves a greater purpose directly. Accountants learning new standards to detect and prevent fraud; lawyers learning how to protect their clients; doctors gaining new insights into how to improve the quality of the care they deliver. The list goes on and on. It's not about the product in these examples, but the big picture outcome. Keeping the purpose alive in your product will result in an emotional connection for your team and for the outside world. This is the super-charger you've been looking for to drive growth and accelerate internal teams.

Ultimately, when associations have a clear ideology with a Core Purpose and Core Values, their products are given greater impor-tance and therefore have more uses. Afterward, it's a matter of explaining to others exactly how the association is living its purpose through its product. If people are not impressed, then go back to the drawing board and figure out how you can either align the associa-tion's purpose and product more distinctly or explain the relationship more clearly.

At Aptify, we wanted our product to embody our purpose, rather than the other way around. It was a critical way to create alignment with our Core Purpose of "Changing the World, One Client Mission at a Time." We were not just selling a service that dozens of others also sold; we were in the business of selling an ideology. That doesn't mean we tossed economics and marketing out the window, of course. We were still a business, after all, and businesses have to make money by selling a product. But it did inspire us to think outside the box more often, because we no longer felt lost if we stepped away from industry norms. Rather than framing our thinking around being a great technology company, we focused on products and services that we felt would advance our clients missions the furthest. This led to some very powerful innovations that wouldn't likely have surfaced if we centered our thinking around technology alone.

The idea of engaging your product's purpose is not all warm and gooey, though. A product can only be as good as your ability to provide it. You have to know what you do best, and you have to be humble enough to acknowledge what someone else does better than you and let go of it. Harvard professor, author, and business consultant, Frances Frei, along with co-author, Anne Morriss, proposed in their book *Uncommon Service,* that organizations should "dare to be bad." Frei and Morriss also note that organizations should admit when they have lost, and know that it's time to walk away when they have.

Take for-profit companies like Wal-Mart and Southwest Airlines as examples. They are excellent at some things, and they're horrible at others. Wal-Mart has excellent pricing, fully stocked shelves, and the convenience of having just about everything you need in one place. But they don't have great ambiance, and they have notoriously bad customer service. Southwest Airlines has a great culture, great customer service, and great pricing, but they have horrible seat selection and no VIP offerings. Neither company pretends to be good at their weak points. But they are fanatical at understanding their core customer, and they make sure they are the best at performing the attributes their core customers find most important. Every organization has weak points. Finding out where yours are is a lot easier if you're willing to look with a critical eye. Everyone connected to your organization will be grateful when you do.

THE EVOLVING NATURE OF COMMUNITY

At an estimated $10 trillion and counting, the 2008 recession was a devastating blow to the American economy. Accounting for total economic losses, from output to unemployment, economists at the Federal Reserve Bank of Dallas estimated that the two-year recession cost every American at least $20,000.[20] Coupled with a large Millennial migration into the workforce at nearly the same time, it was also the most transformative event to hit the American workforce since the Great Depression spit roughly a tenth of all workers into the unemployment line and battered domestic commodity production for generations.

But recently an upside to the 2008 catastrophe has begun to surface, ushering in a new kind of relationship between consumers and businesses. One that's more mindful of saving, shops more consciously, and asks for better ethics from the businesses with which it interacts. The days of super-sized consuming were all but over, as millions of consumers suddenly awakened to debt, joblessness, and

---

20 Tyler Atkinson, David Luttrell, and Harvey Rosenblum, "How Bad Was It? The Cost and Consequences of the 2007-2009 Financial Crisis," *DallasFed: Staff Papers* 20, last modified July 2013, https://www.dallasfed.org/~/media/documents/research/staff/staff1301.pdf.

uncertainty in nearly every aspect of their lives. People began down-sizing and spending less to weather the storm, turning to seemingly antiquated methods of conservation, such as farming their own foods, building their own homes, establishing community sharing programs, and purchasing fewer items of quality rather than large quantities of disposable items. Car owners began keeping their cars for longer than ever before, credit card debt dropped to record lows, and the advancement of technology allowed a new type of **collaborative purchasing** to take place, with shoppers trusting customer reviews far more than marketing campaigns.[21]

Workers that had grown more wary of employers found the online community useful as well, and sites like Glassdoor and Indeed spiked in popularity. Millions began searching for jobs with not just any organization, but rather organizations that their peers could vouch for as well.

The sudden hardships also produced symptoms of greater empathy, evidenced by a wave physical community involvement across the country. Just after the dust from the recession had begun to settle, a 2014 survey from the Corporation for National and Community Service (CNCS) and the National Conference on Citizenship (NCoC) found that roughly one in four Americans volunteered with an organization, more than ever before, and that three out of every five Americans reported informal volunteering by providing labor or financial help to their neighbors, friends, family, or strang-

---

21   Phil LeBeau, "Americans Holding Onto Their Cars Longer Than Ever," CNBC, last modified July 29, 2015, http://www.cnbc.com/2015/07/28/americans-holding-onto-their-cars-longer-than-ever.html; Art Swift, "Americans Rely Less on Credit Cards Than in Previous Years," Gallup, last modified April 25, 2014, http://news.gallup.com/poll/168668/americans-rely-less-credit-cards-previous-years.aspx.

ers.[22] Since 2002, Americans have donated more than 104.9 billion hours of help to others, a number the NCoC values at approximately $2.1 trillion in labor costs.

Americans appeared guarded and disillusioned, but also better connected, informed, and proactive in how they interacted with their society as a whole.

It all says something bigger than we can't currently calculate, offering hints instead at a shift in American values (or perhaps a reinforcement of them) and a reshaping of cultural norms, especially for younger generations.

Societies and the marketplaces that serve them are familiar with evolution, of course. The pillars that hold them have been moving and adapting to change since they were erected. But as much of the world finds itself in a kind of hyper-evolution today, change seems to be asking more from us than it has in recent decades. If associations are to thrive in the future as they have in the past, they must embrace the priorities of the larger communities they knowingly and unknowingly interact with and depend upon. To do so means associations will have to become more of an integrated member of the communities they serve and recruit from.

BRAND COMMUNITIES

Connecting purpose and product ultimately leads to an interesting question: Should associations create their values, purpose, product, and culture around the community they want, or should they find the community that already aligns with them?

---

22   "New Report: 1 in 4 Americans Volunteer; 3 in 5 Help Neighbors," Corporation for National and Community Service, last modified December 8, 2015, https://www.nationalservice.gov/newsroom/press-releases/2015/new-report-1-4-americans-volunteer-3-5-help-neighbors.

Chances are that if you haven't yet discovered your values and purpose, then your culture and the products created within it won't resonate very well with any community. And if an association tries to build its philosophical identity solely around the hopes of attracting a particular community, then it will surely wind up with one that is too disingenuous to motivate anyone, whether inside or outside of the organization's borders.

In *Drive: The Surprising Truth about What Motivates Us*, author Dan Pink outlines three pillars of human motivation:

- Autonomy – A natural wanting for self-determination that, when harnessed properly, transforms compliance into engagement.

- Mastery – The idea that we all have a desire to develop deep expertise in one or more area.

- Purpose – A yearning to do something meaningful and important with our lives. Businesses that are solely focused on profit, and people with no sense of purpose, will not only be very poor at customer service, productivity, and innovation; they will be very unhappy in general.

That last item, purpose, is central to this discussion. People are motivated by authenticity, especially as it relates to purpose. We want to know that the product/service in question will be of good quality, and perhaps the best way of knowing that is by examining whether the organization behind the product/service genuinely believes in it. Aren't we more likely to buy products and services referred to us by someone with whom we share the same purpose and values? Take, for example, the process of hiring a babysitter. Chances are you would rather hire someone you know, or at least someone who a close friend or relative knows well enough to vouch for. It's a similar experience when we make a purchase, whether it's a membership or something material. You might, for instance, decide to buy a new pair of hiking boots because the salesperson is wearing them, or because they tell you that they have the same pair and how well they do in the type of terrain you're planning to trek through next week. We buy into ideas, people, and products based largely on how well they align with our purpose. Genuineness is critical to that perception, and you can't be genuine without first understanding the needs and believing in the same purpose of those you hope to align with.

Brand communities built around lifestyle and culture (e.g., REI, Apple, CrossFit, etc.) are doing exceptionally well today, and the reason behind their success has been their ability to link their product to a larger, more meaningful purpose. Brands capable of connecting people are driven in large part by our innate desire to belong. In an increasingly global society where we are able to interact with others in ways that are relatively limitless compared to decades past, people are seeking out their "tribe" through a shared purpose. We are no longer confined by geography alone, and so our options for finding belonging can now be more specialized. For most businesses, that kind of connectivity also means more competition, meaning brands must focus on their purpose. To do that, organizations should look outside their traditional marketing boundaries to see who they could be engaging with their brand.

You have to know why you're in the space you're in, and what you can do in that space that no one else is doing—ideally finding the things they can't do. Of course, that will require a well-rounded view of client needs and wants and a deep knowledge of the industry itself (i.e., policies, regulations/legislation, etc.), but at the core of everything is finding your overall purpose. Knowing your association's purpose, and the culture connected to it, is vital to developing a product that reflects what you do best. When an organization's purpose defines its product, what it can promise to its members and staff will reveal itself.

But to maintain the momentum of growth, you have to have all your people rethinking the many different things their work does. That's how you continue to move ahead and generate growth, by building on your uniqueness. If you want to be the best, use your courage and creativity to enter uncharted territory and learn. You need to look at what values your members value the most and what attributes they most appreciate. You need to find out what your best peers do better than you and what they do better than anyone. Once you've identified those strengths, see how they do it. What companies do they do business with, what programs do they use, how do they hire, how do they train, how do they market their product? What's appealing about their brand? It's almost always customer service, price, convenience, and quality of the end product, but even the aesthetic elements can go a long way. Hold yourself to the highest standards. And, while you may not be able to meet every one of them every time, you will always find ways to be better than you currently are. Without the excitement of progress and competition, complacency will take hold throughout the organization. Before you know it, you're dead in the water, you're Blockbuster (a once great company that was at first driven by business model innovation, but fell behind rapidly and ultimately failed).

Core Purpose is the beating heart that draws those outside the association in and enlivens those who are already part of the organization, whether it's staff or members.

Core Purpose is the beating heart that draws those outside the association in and enlivens those who are already part of the organization.

As I've said before, associations are poised to take advantage of the power of purpose more than most organizations, as they are already in a rather selfless service to something. Tap into that purpose and use it to stimulate an emotional response in the communities that are, or could be, helped by the association's work. The purpose itself will not only align the association with its members and the communities they belong to, but also make their interactions more rewarding. The more rewarding a person's interaction is, the more frequently they will want to engage with the association. And the more frequently they engage, the more habitual their interactions will become, thus bringing the association greater revenue sustainability with the benefit of a greatly reduced investment of time and resources. In that way, branding based on purpose is a win-win for everyone involved.

CHAPTER WORKSHOP

» All people today have more choices than ever before, thanks in large part to the modern conveniences that technology has made available. Rather than focusing the bulk of your efforts on improving weaknesses (whether they're your own or someone else's), concentrate instead on the options available to outsource those weaknesses somewhere else. Whether it's a piece of technology, a professional, or someone who simply wants to help, you can maximize effort by dropping as many weaknesses as possible and focusing instead on utilizing the strengths. Associations can add value to themselves by helping their members mine for and fortify their strengths, as well as helping them outsource their weaknesses to someone else.

» While we're more connected now than at any time in human history, people still crave community. Group belonging is one of our strongest instincts, and many companies have tapped into that desire by creating brand communities. But they aren't the only ones. Associations are primed for serving as a gathering hub for people to meet and grow together by merging their ideas, services, lifestyles, passions, and needs.

  ▫ How does your association connect people?

  ▫ How does it align products and services to a deeper purpose?

  ▫ Outside of your traditional membership base, who else might find the associations products, services, and knowledge interesting or useful? Chances are, members are only the starting point. With a truly Open Garden, you'll have a massive increase in the potential audience for your expertise.

SUGGESTED READING

Uncommon Service by Frances Frei and Anne Morriss

Chapter Eight

OPEN YOUR GARDEN! SHARING YOUR PURPOSE AND EXPERTISE IN THE DIGITAL AGE

A wealth of information creates a poverty of attention.

—HERBERT A. SIMON

How many commercials have flickered across your television screen advertising a product with the line "Four out of five dentists recommend …"? If you're like me, there have been too many to count. How about the number of times you've seen a billboard or read a news article that references a startling health statistic from the American Heart Association or the American Cancer Society? Have you ever wondered why? It's not surprising that people want to know what the experts know, and in today's seemingly unending content stream, the desire to hear from reliable sources is even greater. That desire puts associations at the center of endless opportunities to take center stage and showcase their work to audiences that would otherwise know nothing about them.

Associations clearly have credibility with their members, but they also have credibility that extends much farther. The Digital Age has delivered all the tools one needs to leverage that credibility by engaging with a large audience more regularly. That's a fact that associations too often don't capitalize on, leaving a valuable and easily accessible market virtually untapped in the process.

A fundamental problem of associations is that their business models have them engaging in deep, but infrequent, ways; a concept also known as **episodic engagement**. Most associations will engage with someone through a seminar, an event, or publication and then remain relatively silent until the next event or publication months later. Those are meaningful forms of engagement. If those are the association's only forms of engagement, however, then it doesn't have the kind of frequency that's needed to build habit or loyalty. The association is not touching people often enough. In order to create that kind of brand habit, an association must compel people (whether members or not) to engage with them frequently and consistently. Doing that requires an association to make its usefulness (i.e., content credibility, quality, topicality, networking value, funding resources, community involvement, etc.) known to as many people as possible, as often as they can.

Alongside the conveniences, the Digital Age has also brought a kind of information overload to the public. We have all been hit with a tidal wave of content, so much so that most people can't make heads or tails of it, because the sheer volume of content and number of sources is overwhelming. At the same time, people are consuming more content than ever before. They're consuming it very rapidly and arguably with less confidence in its credibility than in previous decades.

As a result, most people are not examining the majority of their content in depth. It's impossible to consume every piece of content every day, even the content related to your area, personal interest, or professional field. That's partly driven by the devices we are consuming content on now. People typically aren't reading long-form content as much because they're consuming the majority of content on their mobile phones or computers, where streams of content pour in by the minute, while the nature of the devices promote ADD-like behavior with their constant notifications, vibrations, and sounds. That obviously lends itself well to skimming, but not to in-depth consumption. Unfortunately, that is where most consumers are spending most of their screen time these days. Additionally, mobile use is projected to grow as a percentage of total computing time in the coming years, not decline. All of this means associations need to get in the game and align at least some of their offerings to be mobile-first.

In short, consumers are challenged significantly in filtering out the noise and getting to the right content, and the association faces the problem of episodic (or infrequent) engagement. Associations have highly valued brands, brands with credibility and trust. But too often they fail to use these invaluable assets to their advantage. We have people that are overwhelmed by mostly non-credible content, and we have a credible brand that's looking for a reason to talk to consumers more often. The solution, if not obvious, is content. Consumers want to consume content frequently and they want quite a bit of it. Moreover, they want good, relevant content from trustworthy sources, and they want it tailored to them.

By repositioning the association's brand to provide daily or weekly content to an audience of members and beyond, you're solving a problem for both the individual and the association. The association is giving them the best quality content that's personalized to them, while at the same time asserting its brand value by leveraging its credibility and giving the brand impressions with a target audience on a regular basis, which leads to habit.

Consumers want to consume content frequently and they want quite a bit of it. Moreover, they want good, relevant content from trustworthy sources, and they want it tailored to them.

As I've said before, brand habits form from both frequency of engagement and positive impressions. If you're giving people a redundant email every day that urges them to buy something, they're going to unsubscribe or tune-out and resent the frequency of your messages. However, if you're informing them of something useful or interesting through good-quality and entertaining content, then you have tapped into something with tremendous value.

At rasa.io, we look for macro trends in digital content, using AI to make that objective work at scale. Our algorithms examine consumption patterns by aggregating what people are reading. In other words, we curate content for consumers in a way that directly appeals to them. In deciding the kind of content we send to an individual or group, we first look for topical relevance, where we search for content related to their topics of interest and limit the sources of the content to places the association knows to be trusted and of the highest quality only.

While consumption patterns help a great deal in curating content for people, everyone will inevitably reach a saturation point. For example, when tax reform debates were pulsing through Congress at the end of 2017, many people wanted to read about tax reform. I was one of them, even though I don't have an interest in taxes in general. I had what we call a **situational interest** in content around tax reform, but I also didn't want to read much about it daily, other than what was different from what I previously read. If rasa.io's newsfeed started sending me everything about tax reform every day, I would have found it overwhelming. I don't need the same content from *The New York Times*, *The Wall Street Journal*, *The Economist*, and other sources that basically say, "Here's a summary of the latest version of the tax bill going through the Senate." That wouldn't be interesting to me, but one or two tax reform stories every week or so would.

Topical relevance is only partly what content aggregation software does with algorithms. They also account for situational relevance by looking at what is called an **influencer graph**, which is a variety of methods used to show you content based on the interests of people or organizations you regularly follow online. To do this, the software looks at what people and organizations you trust (based on the regularity with which you read their content or engage with them) and shows you the kind of content they are engaging with, but not necessarily because you're personally seeking out that content.

Another example, **crowd movement**, is the term used for when a large group of people reads a particular piece of content in a specialty field simultaneously. You may see examples of this in your digital information feed, sometimes labeled as "trending" content. This type of AI also looks for patterns using what's called **collaborative filtering**. Collaborative filtering is an algorithmic approach that was first popularized by Amazon for product recommendation. One example I can give is the "diapers and booze" revelation. If you think about content similarity, diapers and booze have nothing to do with each other, right? If I buy diapers, maybe I'm also going to buy something else baby-related, such as baby clothes or food. Using collaborative filtering, retailers figured out that traditional product-similarity cross-selling has significant limitations. They found that once consumers had already added something to a shopping cart that they needed, they were more likely to buy something that they wanted.

For example, if you went out and bought a large quantity of Pampers diapers, are you going to buy Huggies diapers right after that? It doesn't make sense. Researchers found that there was a direct correlation between people buying diapers and people buying alcohol. As diaper consumption increases, so does booze consumption. The products are not related, but the buying pattern is. You can make your own guesses as to why that is, but it's most likely the result of people wanting a kind of treat for doing something they consider work. So, similarly, in the world of content, we can use collaborative filtering to match content to people's interests as well as their situational needs. To put it another way, the software essentially says, "Oh, a lot of people who are reading about tax reform and estate planning are also interested in this third category of content around tropical vacations. Let's give them an article about going to Bora Bora."

That's a simplified example, of course, but the idea around collaborative filtering is centered on behavioral modeling. At rasa.io, we use algorithms to aggregate content based on behavior. Then we blend and reblend these algorithms on a personalized basis to figure out which type of content is most impactful to you. Essentially, we are making guesses, determining that this piece of content is, say, 85 percent likely to be clicked on by you, and 25 percent likely to be clicked on by me. Then, when you actually click on it or don't click on it, we adjust our algorithms dynamically using AI techniques, such as Machine Learning and Deep Learning.

This is not a new concept, nor is it considered groundbreaking in the software world. There has been research and open-source software on collaborative filtering since before Amazon was the online retailing behemoth it is today. Associations are investing in creating **market segments**, which is a contemporary phrase for offering persona-based content. For example, at the American Dental Association, one such persona might be the "young dentist." The ADA might name this persona Susie and ascribe attributes to this fictional consumer. Let's suppose that Susie is thirty-one years old, four years out of dental school, and works for a dental corporation. Let's also suppose that she is one of forty dentists who work in this large office, spends her free time mountain biking or volunteering at a local homeless relief shelter, and makes x amount of dollars annually.

Software algorithms then build a persona based on that information and report back to the ADA something like, "Hey, we think we have 10,000 Susies in the state of Illinois. Let's create a campaign around people like Susie." That type of information helps associations build a more refined consumer model both inside and outside the organization's normal marketing scope.

However, most organizations aren't utilizing these types of digital advantages. If they are using persona-based software to inform their marketing strategies, they are considered a very advanced organization.

Even persona-based marketing falls somewhat flat, because it doesn't really take into account the demographic variances within the proposed segment, nor does it take into account the psychographic differences in individual personality styles. For instance, you might have two Susies that are demographically aligned in terms of age and income, but they have very different personality styles. One might, for example, be an introvert who likes to read books and get their information that way, while the other might be very social who loves going to events and conferences and prefers to get their information that way. The kind of content you present, as well as the kinds of membership opportunities you offer, needs to include a wide range even when using persona-based data.

AI is starting to revolutionize marketing and content in general, because the scale of marketing today and the complexities associated with it requires a really smart computer figuring out what an organization should offer each person. That dilemma is considerably easier for associations, because they already know their members have a very specific interest, such as a particular career field, industry, service, or other issue. That knowledge helps content creators and aggregation software hone in on a type of unifying content.

In 2007, author and futurist, Jim Carroll, released a book called *Ready, Set, Done: How to Innovate When Faster is the New Fast* that argued associations were stuck in a "rut of complacency." Carroll outlines his view by stating that "They [associations] deliver the same old program, focus on the same old issues, generate the same old knowledge, plan the same old conference, and have their agenda managed by the same old membership has-beens.

"They bemoan the fact that membership is declining, that the Millennials have little time or inclination to join them, and the world is becoming too complex to deal with," Carroll writes. "So, they form a committee, hire a consultant, study the issue, and lull themselves into a false sense of future security. By doing so, they are almost guaranteeing themselves a march into oblivion."[23]

Though Carroll is hard on the industry as a whole, he does make some valid points. If an association does not evolve with the changes occurring around it, it certainly cannot define its future. In actuality, it risks becoming obsolete. To avoid falling victim to these perils, associations must be in the business of providing what Carroll dubs "just in time knowledge" to its members. He defines that as the right knowledge at the right time for the right purpose for the right strategy, all revolving around the fact that the knowledge is instant, fast, and transitory.

When people feel like they're getting topical knowledge that comes at the right time offering some sense of future security, people find the content not only to be relevant, but extremely valuable as well. People want information that tells them what they need right now, content that informs them what to do in the next minute, the next day, the next year. Audiences want to consume relevant, credible, useful knowledge quickly, which is why a partnership between associations and AI content aggregators is becoming such a popular tool.

I assume we all want to grow our organizations through sustainable methods. We also want to have a business model that is not contemporary for the sake of being contemporary; to create a sustainable business model that will grow to produce value and a reliable economic future. That's the nature of business, no matter the industry. For associations, that means growing the membership while maintaining the relationships they have with existing members.

---

23 Linton Weeks, "Time For Associations To Trade In Their Past?" NPR, last modified May 25, 2011, https://www.npr.org/2011/05/25/136646070/time-for-associations-to-trade-in-their-past.

Growing membership without alienating current members has to do with frequency. The frequency with which you engage your audience is essentially a prerequisite for habit. Habit formation is the real key to the idea of building enough value for either participant in the relationship to stand the test of time. Though not always the case, membership tends to be annual in nature, but that model is increasingly limiting in today's fast-paced and comparatively commitment-adverse society. Often times, people want to renew monthly or have the option to access a small sample of information whenever they need it without any contract at all. The reasons for a person joining an organization, whether it's a membership model or not, doesn't really matter here. All that matters is the fundamental reason to engage with the brand, which boils down to one question for any audience: Is the content value additive for me?

> *All that matters is the fundamental reason to engage with the brand, which boils down to one question for any audience: Is the content value additive for me?*

In order to get there, the concept of habit formation is critical. If you're forming a positive habit with a consumer, you're building the kind of value for them that makes predicting future content of interest a much easier process. The association, in turn, is also building value for itself in the form of engagement frequency, cross-community visibility, and enhanced credibility through a media outlet using the content as source material.

The other thing about frequency is that data today goes stale much faster than it once did. People's interests change very rapidly in the world we live in today, much more so than even a few years ago and certainly more so than the days when most of us were growing up. Without question, our access to information was far more limited. When you think about those factors, the speed at which data becomes stale or incorrect is so rapid that the degree of engagement frequency ultimately determines not only what the association knows about its audience, but how valuable it is to the audience in question as well. Associations tend to do things that happen infrequently really well (e.g., conferences, annual studies, quarterly news briefs, etc.), but now, more than ever, they must make sure they are doing the little things really frequently (such as curating daily news briefs). People today crave consistency and credibility from their content more than anything else. You have to keep your finger on the pulse of their lives if you hope to provide those cravings for them, as they are looking for somewhere trustworthy they can go to learn about relevant issues on a very immediate basis. That job is one that the association is especially positioned to do very well, because they are already an objective, trusted voice in their field. That alone puts them in a great position to become the master curator for their entire community.

Historically speaking, the decision to join associations was driven in part, or in whole, by a desire to belong or a sense of duty to one's profession. That's really not the case anymore. The Digital Age has given associations an opportunity to remake themselves in a way that is less dependent upon people's social, financial, or professional desire to be part of their organization, all of which are less popular motivators today, due to one's wide access to people, groups, and other resources through technology.

Because it's so important, allow me to reiterate the economic benefits for an association with a highly engaged membership, broader community base, and whose purpose and value are clearly demonstrated and lucrative as well. People who are more aligned with the organization's purpose and more aware of its usefulness are more likely to attend events, recruit others, purchase content, extend memberships, and engage in all other traditional sources of revenue. When people are more frequently thinking about you, they are more likely to support your work.

There is also a revenue model for advertising that's unique to the Digital Age. If you have a platform that people are frequenting regularly because it's meaningful to them, there is a significant opportunity to generate advertising revenue from third parties. By determining someone's interests in certain content, you can better predict their interest in related products and services the association may offer. How so? Well, let's say I've been reading a lot of articles about cyber security lately and there happens to be an association-related webinar coming up next week about cybersecurity. Current technology would allow you to place that information in my news brief.

With this type of digital technology, advertising becomes a bigger source of value for an association, especially for an association with a diverse audience that's more meaningfully engaged. That becomes a revenue stream that could outstrip the revenue streams of perhaps all other revenue sources.

Think about it this way. Let's say my association has fifty thousand members paying x dollars per year. In addition, by embracing the Open Garden Model, we have an audience of non-members that is ten times larger than we've had in the past, all of which are interested in our content and engaged by our brand. That does not mean I am giving up those members. Those fifty thousand members will still be members, but that community of five hundred thousand readers becomes a highly monetizable asset on many levels.

The advertising play is the most obvious one with regard to this category of Digital Age benefits. But benchmarking and selling reports based upon people's interests, habits, and the companies involved in the industry, becomes an incredibly valuable way of leveraging that data and level of audience participation. It's also possible to sell non-members specific offerings such as webinars and education even if they'll never become a member. Rather than thinking that non-members are only valuable if they might be members, organizations need to recognize the value of their brand engaging with anyone interested in their topic of expertise.

Market research becomes a viable way to generate direct economic benefits for the association, simply because it has regular engagement with a large number of people. That fact alone is fundamentally valuable, because the association is now seen as a platform to sell various items and to collect information. These types of **audience monetization** strategies create a sustainable and significant economic engine for the association, and they are dramatically more impactful with a larger audience consisting of members and non-members.

Rather than thinking that non-members are only valuable if they might be members, organizations need to recognize the value of their brand engaging with anyone interested in their topic of expertise.

LEADERSHIP IN A DIGITAL WORLD

With the choices that the digital world has made available and the various changes people are seeing as a result, there's a desire to take wide-ranging choice on board and recognize it as a new constant among many management strategists. The prospect of constant change without any anticipation of it letting up soon is something that frightens many people. That's an understandable fear. This is not just a hurdle to get over after all; it's a mental shift in how we view nearly every aspect of our lives, as well as the lives of those around us. As I've said before, the prospect of losing the comforts of permanent or periodic stillness to a mind-set, in which stability is constantly in motion, doesn't come quietly. When people implicitly recognize that we're moving toward a very dynamic time and will likely be losing a set of circumstances that we are comfortable with, we can expect that problems adapting to these changes won't be far behind.

People talk about a **digital transformation** (a Sci-Fi-esque genesis in which people and businesses will forever be changed once digital technology sweeps across every aspect of human civilization) more today than they used to, even more than they did during the dot-com bubble. Individuals and organizations are both engaging with technology more and more every day. And, as I'm sure you already know, conversations grow louder when more voices attach to them. Some of those voices say that this a total digital transformation. Others see it as a time to invest and cash in on the action, a kind of gold rush, but with apps and tablets instead of pans and sluice boxes. Others believe this is all just a passing trend, and everyone will move on as soon as the next big innovation comes along.

For me, though, the expansion of choice and the dynamics of a connected world is somewhere in between. Digital technology today is certainly a more important development than the time Betamax met the VHS. Like most, I see the digital elements as the drivers of so much of the change we're seeing in society and business today, but humans will still be very much the same when the dust settles. The questions before us now include how and where an organization starts to incorporate and integrate both the technology and the ideas that come with it. The answers are a fundamental requirement if one is going to be an integrated part of the modern world.

Perhaps we can examine this crossroads with a little reference to physics. Inertia is a compelling challenge when it comes to driving change. The effort required to get a static giant (such as a large organization) moving is huge. The larger the organization, the more effort needed to accommodate the growing number of choices in the way it approaches its work. Keep in mind that stagnation is a choice, although it sometimes feels more like an inability to move than a decision to stay put. But in this case, the decision to act must be made, and that decision should be recognized and understood by all, so everyone is aware of the future path they've decided to embark upon. This is why incremental change and experimentation are so critical in organizations of all sizes. Innovation can't easily happen in large doses unless you're constantly in a state of tinkering and learning.

> *This is why incremental change and experimentation are so critical in organizations of all sizes. Innovation can't easily happen in large doses unless you're constantly in a state of tinkering and learning.*

An organization should be able to communicate to everyone involved what the choice to act on technology fully means. There will be many options now and many elements later on that will all be changing rapidly. Directions and decisions are required for each. They don't necessarily need to be done at the same time; many are interdependent, but they will require thoughtful decisions and regular tracking and updating.

To utilize the newly afforded power of choice in the best ways, leaders have to understand all the different places that it touches.

Those in leadership have to thoroughly examine the pieces that have to do with culture, workplace flexibility, engagement, collaboration, community, and the membership framework in general. All of these elements are part and parcel of different things that are interwoven into the organization's fabric.

Drastic changes may be necessary as new developments arise, whether it's new tech-enabled choices that spring up or the mind-sets that come along with them. How well an organization leads through them will depend on how well its leaders track and adjust to the changes attached to choice. The kind of policies in place, what your values are, why you exist, how you're going to deal with an evolving, expanding workforce and member base—all of these questions need to be prioritized.

To be successful, leaders should talk about what one's looking at. You need to be able to identify the legacy habits that are no longer conducive to the current environment and ensure that they aren't included in any future policies. Taking a particular principle and doing a beta test with it in the current landscape can do that. Once you have a good understanding of the results, you should choose the principles that worked and seem likely to be useful in the future to include in your decision-making process going forward.

So again, choosing a structure that is going to be very fixed is not going to work in the future. You will need a framework that allows you to pivot quickly when making decisions or adapting to changes, lest you be stuck with traditional habits that can't propel you upward.

CHAPTER WORKSHOP

» The modern age has people consuming content in enormous quantities, whether it's articles, images, social media posts, videos, or music. With the growing abundance of content availability, people are also consuming content with a great deal of choice in its source. The challenge is no longer a lack of content; the challenge now is providing users with quality content from trustworthy sources that they find relevant to them. Associations can use technology to monetize their expertise through a number of different concepts and tools.

- **Audience monetization.** Any strategy that seeks to add a revenue stream to the organization by capitalizing on the interaction users have with its content, such as selling digital ads, subscriptions, product reviews, etc. Audience monetization strategies are more successful and profitable in larger audience bases with an array of interests, thus why they should seek to include members and non-members alike.

- **Situational interest.** The concept that a user is only casually or temporarily interested in a topic, usually due to the user's needs or wants at a specific period in time (e.g., a user's interest in tax-related content in the months or weeks prior to major tax deadlines, etc.).

- **Influencer graph.** A data-set that is used to determine who people are influenced by the most. The most commonly referenced one is the follower/following relationship on Twitter, however, Influencer graphs exist in many places.

- **Crowd movement.** A tactic that allows an organization to track the popularity of a specific piece of content among its readers.

- **Market segments.** Fairly new in terms of widespread adoption, persona-based content, or market segments, allow organizations to target a specific group of users based on common demographical information, such as geography, age, occupation, gender, etc.

- **Frequency.** Frequency builds habit, and frequency is driven by one's need or desire to engage with the brand. The more useful, enjoyable, and valuable the content, the more habit-forming the brand will be. Users who are more aligned with the organization's purpose are more likely to attend events, recruit others, consume and purchase content, extend memberships, and all other traditional sources of revenue. The more often the organization is in the user's line of sight, the more opportunities there are to prove its importance to the user's life.

SUGGESTED READING

Ready, Set, Done: How to Innovate When Faster is the New Fast by Jim Carroll

Chapter Nine

MAINTAINING YOUR GARDEN

We are what we repeatedly do. Excellence,
then, is not an act, but a habit.

—ARISTOTLE

A few years into Aptify's journey toward rebooting its culture, we noticed a problem. As we talked to clients about when they were successful and when they weren't, we did so partly because we wanted to find common themes among each client's successes and challenges. One of the most common challenges our clients told us about was their inability to maintain a strong IT or technology staff in their association. That remains a big challenge in the industry to this day. Hiring IT people is competitive in general, and associations aren't necessarily the most attractive place for these types of folks to work for a number of reasons. For one, associations are usually not financially competitive with the companies in the private sector, rendering them unable to match or beat salary and benefits packages. For another, most IT people like to be around other IT people, and most associations only have a handful of these folks working there.

We had listened to these challenges before, and in our old way of thinking about it, we couldn't see how we might be able to solve the problem. Our mission statement was focused on "the full potential through flexible technology and world-class service," so, while the problem was interesting to us, we viewed it as an external force that affected everyone in the industry. Because of that limiting viewpoint, it was neither our problem nor was there anything we could do about it.

That perspective changed as soon as we discovered our Core Purpose and shifted to an Open Garden approach with the aim of "changing the world, one client mission at a time." By recalibrating ourselves around the idea of advancing our clients' missions and being completely void of the idea of a specific product or set of products or services, all we needed to guide our daily decision-making was to ask ourselves the questions, "How can we fix that problem? Is there a way to think creatively in fixing that problem?" By forgetting about who we were and the products we sold, the boundaries we had once placed around ourselves allowed us to transform into a company that could do much more than our competitors and even our initial ambitions.

Over the last decade, there has been a strong movement toward

> *By forgetting about who we were and the products we sold, the boundaries we had once placed around ourselves allowed us to transform into a company that could do much more than our competitors and even our initial ambitions.*

purposeful business. If you think about books like 2013's *Conscious Capitalism*, by John Mackey and Rajendra Sisodia, or the movement around the so-called "evergreen companies" (which design themselves to remain independent and purpose focused indefinitely), and triple-bottom line (or 3L) companies (which use a three-part accounting framework to measure the social, environmental, and financial impacts of the company), it's clear that many incredible things are happening in the ways businesses interact with society itself. At their center, ideas and actions like these are all very exciting manifestations of purposefulness.

That's great, but it's harder to get these practices into the mainstream, because they are, well, "squishy." Ideas like purposefulness, social responsibility, and so forth don't directly tie to the bottom line, at least not in a way that's immediately observable. In traditional business school—and even for those who don't go to business school—we hear that the purpose of business is to maximize shareholder value or shareholder wealth. It's that simple, really. According to traditional views on business, the entire purpose of the company is inward-facing, focusing more on putting and keeping things in as opposed to thinking too much about what it's putting or keeping out.

That view is starting to change, but for many who learned the purpose of business in the traditional sense, it's easy to miss the full benefits of Open Garden's Purpose + Culture + Inclusivity model. If a

> *According to traditional views on business, the entire purpose of the company is inward-facing, focusing more on putting and keeping things in as opposed to thinking too much about what it's putting or keeping out.*

person has a deeply ingrained, but narrow view of their purpose, then everything else is a plus, right? They're not capable of thinking about their full impact any more than they are of realizing their full potential. As a result, many business leaders believe that culture is important to the extent that it drives profitability. I maintain that profitability is a wonderful byproduct if you have a culture that is not only meaningful, deep, and consistent, but one that is genuine and not manufactured in order to say that you have one.

Whenever I talk to an entrepreneur, business owner, or association executive, I will ask them to tell me about their culture. Across the board, I hear about things that aren't truly connected to culture at all. "Oh, it's great!" they might say, beaming. "We've got Foosball tables. We've got a slide in our office. We've got free pizza on Fridays and events for beer buffs every other weekend."

That's all great stuff. There's nothing necessarily wrong with making a workplace comfortable and fun, but that's not culture. Those are fringe benefits. Those are things that help boost engagement, but it doesn't say anything about why people are there in the first place. Why people are there is the foundation of culture. If someone's only there because there's a Foosball table and they get a free slice of pizza on occasion, then you won't be able to motivate them for very long and you certainly won't be able to inspire their work. Without an understanding of what your purpose, values, and visions for the future are people will never feel rooted in anything that drives them to do more than the minimum. For associations, if the minimum is

For associations, if the minimum is nothing (i.e., to join or not to join, to volunteer or not to volunteer), then the communities they depend on are more likely to do nothing to help them.

nothing (i.e., to join or not to join, to volunteer or not to volunteer), then the communities they depend on are more likely to do nothing to help them.

Even when an association does discover its purpose, define its values, strengthen its capacities, and find success in serving something larger than its members, unfortunately the journey is still not over. Keeping it all running smoothly depends on how well each element stays aligned with the other. Doing so requires a constant reinforcement of your purpose and values through your daily decisions.

Associations form out of their members, so obviously everyone wants to maximize benefits to the membership. But with Open Garden, you ultimately drive more value to members by thinking more broadly about how the association's work affects the wider population. The more aware people are of the association's value, the more aware they are of its members' value as well. The association is also able to profit from the larger audience as we have discussed previously, creating a larger and more sustainable financial model which can in turn be used to advance purpose even further.

Additionally, once you understand how the work you're doing affects the broader population, why the association (and perhaps you) exists is much easier to understand. We have covered the concept of Core Purpose in the preceding chapters, but maintaining it is a matter of how you, as an individual,

But with Open Garden, you ultimately drive more value to members by thinking more broadly about how the association's work affects the wider population. The more aware people are of the association's value, the more aware they are of its members' value as well.

set your priorities. While your purpose should be expansive, your priorities should be narrow, focusing on the small steps that are necessary toward fulfilling your commitment to Core Purpose every day. Once you define a clear purpose statement, then as you operationalize it, you should feel that you're testing it every day. You're not just affirming it in staff meetings or annual and quarterly planning sessions; you're operationalizing it every day through your work.

That's what made the culture at Aptify work so well, and why rasa.io is off to a strong start, because every day people talk about Core Purpose and if designs are supporting the Core Purpose or not. We used many instruments in our culture to reinforce our momentum once that began, but I'll give you one example from the executive level. When we think about products and services, if you start by saying that you're a technology company, a services company, or something else, then you're guaranteed to repeat the same stuff as someone else. But if you start with an explanation of your Core Purpose, then you come up with more creative ideas, because you can test whether or not things are actually improving.

The real value of the Open Garden Model is not just about selling what's in your stock; it's about expanding what you can offer and to whom you can offer it. The goal is to use the association's expertise more like an electromagnet than a megaphone to attract people. Remember that membership isn't the only path forward. Engaging a broader audience increases the association's brand equity, and it affords a higher level of useful insights, revenue streams, and talents by including more people who care about the associa-

> *The real value of the Open Garden Model is not just about selling what's in your stock; it's about expanding what you can offer and to whom you can offer it.*

tion's topic of expertise. It's a virtuous cycle that will only strengthen the association as the community expands. In whatever direction you take, whatever your purpose is, as long as you lead with your values in pursuit of a meaningful purpose, I'm confident you'll like where you arrive. We can all do better. Let's start today.

CHAPTER WORKSHOP

» **Believe in your purpose.** Ask why the association exists as many times as it takes to get to the heart of its work. A Core Purpose should evoke an emotional response in people, so ask members and staff how they feel about the association's purpose. Does it inspire them? Do they believe it will make a positive difference in the world? Are they willing to help pursue it?

» **Live your purpose daily.** Whether you're an executive or a volunteer, how does your day-to-day work within the business reinforce the association's purpose? Can you test every major and minor decision against its alignment with your purpose? If so, are you making the grade?

» **Stand by your values.** Once Core Values are discovered and defined, it must be absolutely mandatory for everyone at all levels to be aligned with them. You can't teach Core Values; either someone is naturally aligned with the organization's value system or they are not. Hire for attitude and aptitude, and train for skills. Along with refusing to fire people whose Core Values are misaligned, hiring for skills alone is the number one mistake leaders make in building and maintaining a commitment to Core Values. Without that collective commitment, a major pillar of the Open Garden Model will crumble, endangering the success of the association's purpose and growth.

» **Grow sustainable revenue** by including a larger audience. Allowing more people to learn from and contribute to the association only bolster's its value, leading to more new memberships sold, more renewals, more conference attendees, better market research, larger data collection, and more engaged audience with habitual-use tendencies that generate higher ad and sponsorship revenues.

» **Narrow your priorities.** Establish a set of small priorities and goals (whether daily, weekly, monthly, yearly, or beyond) that will keep you moving toward your purpose. Create an organizational rhythm that supports these priorities at all levels by constantly reminding everyone of the organization's Core Purpose and Core Values. You will get much farther with a community of supporters who are committed to the core importance of the association than you will with a group of individuals who are only committed to furthering themselves.

SUGGESTED READING

Conscious Capitalism by John Mackey and Rajendra Sisodia

Association Success Companies

AssociationSuccess.org

AssociationSuccess.org is a platform for association professionals to connect, learn, and share ideas for innovation. Associations have a massive potential to make a positive impact on the world and AssociationSuccess.org provides a unique online platform for discussing disruptive technology, new business models and engagement techniques, and anything else that can drive an organization's mission forward.

AssociationSuccess.org provides free content, virtual conferences, and education resources.

rasa.io

rasa.io is committed to rethinking how associations can thrive as digital brands and take full advantage of Artificial Intelligence in all of its forms. Our first product generates an automated newsletter for associations to share the best content for each of their members in a personalized manner. Our AI finds the best content in the world from sources each association considers trustworthy, and then picks several articles for each individual that are truly aligned with their interests and personality. The result is a far more relevant newsletter that each recipient will find value in. As we continue to grow and help associations, we aim to become "the AI company for associations" and provide a wide array of solutions that help our clients dramatically accelerate their missions.

We are rethinking how associations can flourish digitally and take full advantage of Artificial Intelligence in developing their missions. Together with AssociationSuccess.org, we are rallied around a single purpose: to help associations thrive and succeed in today's ever-changing environment. Learn more at www.rasa.io.

Connect with Amith to learn more
about his role in these two companies.
Visit him on **LinkedIn** at **www.linkedin.com/in/amithnagarajan/**
or on **Twitter @amithnagarajan.**